First World War
and Army of Occupation
War Diary
France, Belgium and Germany

40 DIVISION
Headquarters, Branches and Services
Royal Army Ordnance Corps
Deputy Assistant Director Ordnance Services
3 January 1916 - 30 April 1919

WO95/2597/3

The Naval & Military Press Ltd
www.nmarchive.com
Published in association with The National Archives

Published by

The Naval & Military Press Ltd

Unit 10 Ridgewood Industrial Park,

Uckfield, East Sussex,

TN22 5QE England

Tel: +44 (0) 1825 749494

www.naval-military-press.com

www.nmarchive.com

This diary has been reprinted in facsimile from the original. Any imperfections are inevitably reproduced and the quality may fall short of modern type and cartographic standards.

© Crown Copyright
Images reproduced by permission of The National Archives, London, England, 2015.

Contents

Document type	Place/Title	Date From	Date To
Heading	WO95/2597/3		
Heading	D.A. Dir. Ordnance Serv. Jun 1916-Apr 1919		
Miscellaneous	D.A.G. 3rd Echelon		
War Diary	Lillers	01/06/1916	01/06/1916
War Diary	Lillers	03/01/1916	03/01/1916
War Diary	Lillers	03/06/1916	18/06/1916
War Diary	Bruay	19/06/1916	30/06/1916
Miscellaneous	Headquarters, 40th Division	21/08/1916	21/08/1916
War Diary	Bruay	01/07/1916	03/07/1916
War Diary	Noeux Les Mines	04/07/1916	30/10/1916
War Diary	Roellecourt	31/10/1916	03/11/1916
War Diary	Fndronle Grand	04/11/1916	04/11/1916
War Diary	Berneville	05/11/1916	16/11/1916
War Diary	Frohen Le Grand	16/11/1916	18/11/1916
War Diary	Bouquemaison	19/11/1916	22/11/1916
War Diary	Doullens	23/11/1916	23/11/1916
War Diary	Canaples	24/11/1916	24/11/1916
War Diary	Ailly Le Haut Clocher	25/11/1916	15/12/1916
War Diary	Chipilly	16/12/1916	28/12/1916
War Diary	Bray Sur Somme	29/12/1916	27/01/1917
War Diary	Chipilly	28/01/1917	11/02/1917
War Diary	Bray Sur Somme	12/02/1917	21/02/1917
War Diary	Curlu	22/03/1917	07/04/1917
War Diary	Bouchevenes	08/04/1917	19/04/1917
War Diary	Moislains	20/04/1917	03/05/1917
War Diary	Fins	04/05/1917	08/10/1917
War Diary	Beaumetz Les Loges	09/10/1917	30/10/1917
War Diary	Mondicourt	31/10/1917	05/11/1917
War Diary	Gombremetz	06/11/1917	14/11/1917
War Diary	La Herliere	15/11/1917	17/11/1917
War Diary	Beauhencourt	18/11/1917	26/11/1917
War Diary	Beaumetz Les Loges	27/11/1917	02/12/1917
War Diary	Ervillers	03/12/1917	12/02/1918
War Diary	Boiry St Rictrude	13/02/1918	18/02/1918
War Diary	Beaumetz Les Fogie	01/03/1918	13/03/1918
War Diary	Boiry St Rectrude	14/03/1918	22/03/1918
War Diary	Afender	23/03/1918	24/03/1918
War Diary	Bucquoy Souastre Hannes Camp	25/03/1918	26/03/1918
War Diary	Pommiers	26/03/1918	26/03/1918
War Diary	Saulty	27/03/1918	31/03/1918
War Diary	Merville	01/04/1918	02/04/1918
War Diary	Cnl de Sac Farm	03/04/1918	08/04/1918
War Diary	Vieux Berquin.	09/04/1918	09/04/1918
War Diary	Strozeele Hazebrouck	10/04/1918	13/04/1918
War Diary	Ebblinghem	14/04/1918	14/04/1918
War Diary	La Martin An Forest	15/04/1918	21/04/1918
War Diary	Wizernes	22/04/1918	13/05/1918
War Diary	Ebblinghem	14/05/1918	24/08/1918
War Diary	Wallon Cappel	25/08/1918	30/08/1918
War Diary	Hazebruck	31/08/1918	03/09/1918

War Diary	Near La Motte	04/09/1918	16/09/1918
War Diary	Steenwerck	17/09/1918	19/09/1918
War Diary	Armentieres	20/09/1918	21/09/1918
War Diary	Wambrechies	22/09/1918	28/09/1918
War Diary	Lannoy	29/09/1918	30/09/1918
Miscellaneous	D.A.G. 40th Divn	30/11/1918	30/11/1918
War Diary	Lannoy	01/11/1918	26/11/1918
War Diary	Roubaix	27/11/1918	30/04/1919

WO 95/2597/3

40TH DIVISION

D. A. DIR. ORDNANCE SERV.

JUN 1916 – APR 1919

F.A. 3rd October

Received my dear Sir Mr North
of June. I entirely agree with some of
his views & activities of my statements
and so send w??

Sincerely yours
D.A.R??

2/7/6

WAR DIARY
or
INTELLIGENCE SUMMARY
(Erase heading not required.)

Army Form C. 2118

Instructions regarding War Diaries and Intelligence Summaries are contained in F. S. Regs., Part II. and the Staff Manual respectively. Title Pages will be prepared in manuscript.

Place	Date	Hour	Summary of Events and Information	Remarks and references to Appendices
Lillers	1/6/16		Dump Selected. Rue St Hauwinville near Railway Station. Visited D.A.D.O.S. 12th Div on Lillers & saw 12th Div Dump. Called on Town Major re Billeting & workshop accomodation. Afternoon motored over area allocated to 45th Div with D.A.A & Q.M.G. Selected workshop accomodation in Rue de Bethune	
			C.W. Hermes Capt & D.A.D.O.S. 45th Div	

1875 Wt. W593/826 1,000,000 4/15 J.B.C. & A. A.D.S.S./Forms/C. 2118.

WAR DIARY or INTELLIGENCE SUMMARY

Place	Date	Hour	Summary of Events and Information	Remarks and references to Appendices
Lillers	3/1/16		Secured fatigue party and cleared barns at Dump of wood etc.	
			Hired Trestles & Trestle tops for office, Handcart, Tables & chairs etc.	
			Motored to La Boussière to see A.D.O.S 1st Corps	
			Wired Calais names of Units of 40th Division in order of embarkation.	
			Motored to Noeux-les-Mines to see DADOS of 16th Division — Examined system etc in practice.	

W McInnis Capt
DADOS 40th Divn

WAR DIARY
or
INTELLIGENCE SUMMARY
(Erase heading not required.)

Army Form C. 2118

Instructions regarding War Diaries and Intelligence Summaries are contained in F. S. Regs., Part II. and the Staff Manual respectively. Title Pages will be prepared in manuscript.

Place	Date	Hour	Summary of Events and Information	Remarks and references to Appendices
Lillers	3/6/15		Decided to have office in small marquee if such could be obtained & pitch adjacent to Dump in orchard. Obtained permission & borrowed a small marquee & two C S L Tents from D A D O S 16th Div. Visited Signalling Officer and arranged for Telephone to be installed. Afternoon motored to Head Qr 1st Army at aire to see D.D.O.S. & obtain copies of G R O's.	

McGuinness Capt
D A D O S 40th Div.

1875 Wt. W593/826 1,000,000 4/15 J.B.C. & A. A.D.S.S./Forms/C. 2118.

WAR DIARY
or
INTELLIGENCE SUMMARY
(Erase heading not required.)

Army Form C. 2118

Place	Date	Hour	Summary of Events and Information	Remarks and references to Appendices
Lillers	4/6/16		Visited No 2 4 Workshop at La Bouvière with A.D.O.S. 1st Corps & returned with him to La Boussière — Motored to Noeux-les-Mines to see D.A.D.O.S 16th Division. On return pitched Marquee in readiness for arrival of Staff following day.	

LeDiennes Capt
D.A.D.O.S. 4th Div

WAR DIARY
or
INTELLIGENCE SUMMARY
(Erase heading not required.)

Army Form C. 2118

Instructions regarding War Diaries and Intelligence Summaries are contained in F. S. Regs., Part II. and the Staff Manual respectively. Title Pages will be prepared in manuscript.

Place	Date	Hour	Summary of Events and Information	Remarks and references to Appendices
Lillers	5/4/16		A.O.C. Staff arrived Lillers — withdrew Brigade Warrant officers to Headquarters. Pitched two C.S.t tents, & made office arrangements took over Billets & Indented for Rations. Visited Headqrs in afternoon.	
				Mc Kenzies Capt. *D.A.D.O.S 45th Div*

1875 Wt. W593/826 1,000,000 4/15 J.B.C. & A. A.D.S.S./Forms/C. 2118.

WAR DIARY or INTELLIGENCE SUMMARY

Army Form C. 2118

(Erase heading not required.)

Place	Date	Hour	Summary of Events and Information	Remarks and references to Appendices
Lillers	6/6/16		Motored Conductor Hilton & Sub Conductor Chadwick to Head Qrs 16th Division to examine system as worked by that Division. Ascertained from Head Qrs 1st Army that system & methods there are considered good by them. C. Battery 178th Brigade notified that they had two damaged guns. (i.e. Rocking Bar Sight & Traversing Gear). Ordered guns to No 24 Workshop La Boussière. Sent Lorry to fetch 8 3" Trench mortars from La Boussière (Head Qrs 1st Corps) & 1 C.L.L Tents for Head Qrs Div Artillery. Issued circular memoranda to all units of 40th Divn as to days for demanding & drawing stores. Sent first Buck線 Trench mortars allocated as follows 4 to Head Qrs 119th Infantry Brigade, 4 to Head Qrs 120th Infantry Brigade.	

G.W. Dennis Capt
D.A.D.O.S 40th Divn

WAR DIARY
or
INTELLIGENCE SUMMARY
(Erase heading not required.)

Army Form C. 2118

Instructions regarding War Diaries and Intelligence Summaries are contained in F. S. Regs., Part II. and the Staff Manual respectively. Title Pages will be prepared in manuscript.

Place	Date	Hour	Summary of Events and Information	Remarks and references to Appendices
Lillers	7/6/16		Issued the 8 Trench Mortars referred to in diary 6/6/16. A.D.O.S 1st Corps called at 2-30 p.m. Went to Mercat Pule's Head Qrs in afternoon to see A.a.&.Q.M.G. Later in afternoon drew 1000 frs from Field Cashier. In Imprest a/c — Hastened steel Helmets from Calais and made arrangements through A.D.O.S to borrow 1500 from 12th Division for present needs with 1500 more in reserve if required. arranged with C.R.E. to issue 2 Sandbags per man to the Bantam Battalions before moving up into the line.	

En Siennes Capt.
D.A.D.O.S 4 8th Div.

1875 Wt. W593/826 1,000,000 4/15 J.B.C. & A. A.D.S.S./Forms/C. 2118.

WAR DIARY or INTELLIGENCE SUMMARY

Army Form C. 2118

Place	Date	Hour	Summary of Events and Information	Remarks and references to Appendices
Lillers	8/6/16		Fetched 1500 Steel Helmets from La Bouvriere and issued 150 to 231st Field Coy RE = Secured 12 gross of Safety Pins for Gas Helmets through A.D.O.S 1st Corps from O.O. Ordnance Dump La Bouvriere & 70 Gas (P.H.) Helmets on loan from D.A.D.O.S 16 Divn Noeux-les-Mines. Calais advise 3950 Helmets en route - also 29 cases Helmets Flannel.	

Ardiennes Capt
D.A.D.O.S 46th Divn

WAR DIARY
or
INTELLIGENCE SUMMARY
(Erase heading not required.)

Army Form C. 2118

Instructions regarding War Diaries and Intelligence Summaries are contained in F. S. Regs., Part II. and the Staff Manual respectively. Title Pages will be prepared in manuscript.

Place	Date	Hour	Summary of Events and Information	Remarks and references to Appendices
Lillers	9/6/16		Lieut Lancaster joined on orders from the ADOS 1st Army. Steel Helmets issued to units going up to first line by Lorry (10 miles) Total amount issued to date 3049. 3950 Steel Helmets en route from Calais. Issued Safety pins (3 per man) to all units going up to firing line. Issues of Steel Helmets & Safety Pins to. Head Qrs 119th Brigade 19th Royal Welch Fusiliers 17th Welch Regt 2 Coys 12th Yorkshire Regt. (Pioneers) 229th Field Coy R.E. Indiennes Cap. D.H.D.O.S 40th Divn	

1875   Wt. W593/826   1,000,000   4/15   J.B.C. & A.   A.D.S.S./Forms/C. 2118.

Place	Date	Hour	Summary of Events and Information	Remarks and references to Appendices
Sillers	10/6/16		Received 3950 Steel Helmets from Calais also 29 Cases of P.H. Gas Helmets.	
			Issued Steel Helmets to 1 Coy 12th Yorkshire (Pioneers) also Safety Pins.	
			Motored to La Boussière. Re Safety Pins saw A.D.O.S.	

Andrews Capt
D.A.D.O.S 48th Div

WAR DIARY
or
INTELLIGENCE SUMMARY
(Erase heading not required.)

Army Form C. 2118

Instructions regarding War Diaries and Intelligence Summaries are contained in F. S. Regs., Part II. and the Staff Manual respectively. Title Pages will be prepared in manuscript.

Place	Date	Hour	Summary of Events and Information	Remarks and references to Appendices
Lillers	11/6/16		Issued Steel Helmets to Head qrs 120th Brigade 14th H.L.I. 11th Kings own Lancaster Regt. at Bethune also Safety Pins. Received from D.A.D.O.S 12th Divn 70 Latrine Buckets & from O.A. Calais 257 Cases of Gas Helmets & 21 Cases of Goggles.	

Cusiennis Capt.
D.A.D.O.S 40th Divn

1875 Wt. W593/826 1,000,000 4/15 J.B.C. & A. A.D.S.S./Forms/C. 2118.

Place	Date	Hour	Summary of Events and Information	Remarks and references to Appendices
Lillers	12/6/16		Issued 150 Steel Helmets to 224 Coy RE. Secured 400 more Steel Helmets from No 24 Workshop La Bouvrière. Attended Divisional Staff Conference 5.30 PM Routine work etc.	

G W Lewis Capt
DADOS 40th Div

WAR DIARY
or
INTELLIGENCE SUMMARY
(Erase heading not required.)

Army Form C. 2118

Instructions regarding War Diaries and Intelligence Summaries are contained in F. S. Regs., Part II. and the Staff Manual respectively. Title Pages will be prepared in manuscript.

Place	Date	Hour	Summary of Events and Information	Remarks and references to Appendices
Lillers	13/6/16		Ordered to hand over 5 Trench Mortars (3") recently issued to 119th & 120th Brigades, to 12th Division. Notified by Calais that 14 Cases of Trench Mortars had been despatched (2") these when received are to be handed over to Trench Mortar School. Issued 1929 Steel Helmets to 12th S.W.B. 18th Welch Regt. & 50 to R.E.a. also 5787 Safety Pins to 18th Welch & 12th S.W.B. Notified receipt of 12 pairs of wheels at OZ Railhead. Motored to La Boisserie for Safety Pins supplied by I.C. Corps Ordnance Dump.	

Onsicuries Capt
D.A.D.O.S. 40th Div.

1875 Wt. W593/826 1,000,000 4/15 J.B.C. & A. A.D.S.S./Forms/C. 2118.

Place	Date	Hour	Summary of Events and Information	Remarks and references to Appendices
Lillers	14/6/16		Bulk Stores Truck 33953 arrived at Choques containing Screens Latrines - Head & Heel Ropes - Buckets Canvas etc etc. Fetched 12 2" Trench Mortars from Trench Mortar School at St Venant. Issued Helmets Gas S.P. to 12th S.W.B. 19th Welch Fusiliers & to 17th & 18th Welch Regts. Went to Bethune on Local Purchase - arranged transfer of 8 3" Stokes Trench Mortars from 119th & 120th Brigades which had not been sent in according to instructions to D.A.D.O.S 12th Division.	

CW Dieuines Capt
D.A.D.O.S 40th Div.

WAR DIARY
or
INTELLIGENCE SUMMARY
(Erase heading not required.)

Army Form C. 2118

Instructions regarding War Diaries and Intelligence Summaries are contained in F. S. Regs., Part II. and the Staff Manual respectively. Title Pages will be prepared in manuscript.

Place	Date	Hour	Summary of Events and Information	Remarks and references to Appendices
Lillers	15/6/16		Fetched 4 Tons of general stores from Railhead also 3650 Steel Helmets. Motored in afternoon to Heavy Mobile Workshops Merville & took Lewis from magazines there for repair. Saw I.O.M re French Carts & secured a promise of early delivery. Returned to Lillers & from there motored to Norrent Fontes (Head qrs 48th Divn) to see D.A.D.M.S.	

A.H. Lennis Capt
D.A.D.O.S. 48th Divn

1875 Wt. W593/826 1,000,000 4/15 J.B.C. & A. A.D.S.S./Forms/C. 2118.

No 16

WAR DIARY or INTELLIGENCE SUMMARY

Army Form C. 2118

Place	Date	Hour	Summary of Events and Information	Remarks and references to Appendices
Lillers	14/8/16		Received a Truck of General Stores (2 Tons) containing Helmets P.H.G. Sager Stoves &c. Received orders to take over Store, Workshops &c from D.A.D.O.S 12th Div'n. Went to Choques took over co-ordnce. Went to Head Qrs 1st Corps asked A.D.A.Q.M.G. to allow me to move Dump Workshops &c to Bruay. He consented and took to Bruay saw Town Major secured suitable officies, Dump &c arranged billets and arranged to move the following day. Ordered to hand over the ~~Light Trench~~ Mortars issued to 40th Div'n to 12th Div'n.	W.S. Lewis Capt D.A.D.O.S 40th Div

| | | | WAR DIARY or INTELLIGENCE SUMMARY (Erase heading not required.) | Army Form C. 2118 |

Instructions regarding War Diaries and Intelligence Summaries are contained in F. S. Regs., Part II. and the Staff Manual respectively. Title Pages will be prepared in manuscript.

Place	Date	Hour	Summary of Events and Information	Remarks and references to Appendices
Lillers	17/6/16		Started moving from Lillers to Bruay (10 miles) Sent Lorries (4) to Chocques (railhead) to get cases of Steel Helmets Brassdoes & Bicycles & take to Ordnance Store - Bruay. Got Shoemakers tools & leather over from DADOS 12th & sent to Bruay. Sent Lorry to Noeux les Mines to get 24 cases containing 3" Trench mortars. these to be taken on to Bruay - (allocation to be made to the 3 Infantry Brigades 8 each). Colonel Tufnell C.B. DDOS Communications Base North called, obtained permission from him to wire for an N.C.O. for Railhead. Demanded an allotments of tents from 1st Corps according to Divisional Instructions.	
			W Lewis Capt DADOS 40th Div n	

1875 Wt. W593/826 1,000,000 4/15 J.B.C. & A. A.D.S.S./Forms/C. 2118.

WAR DIARY or INTELLIGENCE SUMMARY

Place	Date	Hour	Summary of Events and Information	Remarks and references to Appendices
Lillers	10/6/16		Struck Tents - packed up & loaded remainder of Stores & transferred to Bruay from Lillers - Lieut Lancaster went to Bruay & received stores.	

McInnes Capt
DADOS 47th Div

WAR DIARY
or
INTELLIGENCE SUMMARY
(Erase heading not required.)

Army Form C. 2118

Instructions regarding War Diaries and Intelligence Summaries are contained in F. S. Regs., Part II. and the Staff Manual respectively. Title Pages will be prepared in manuscript.

Place	Date	Hour	Summary of Events and Information	Remarks and references to Appendices
Bmay	19/6/16		Opened Ordnance Dump. Issued 1000 Steel Helmets to 20th & 21st Middlesex (500 each Batt) Brought in from Railhead 5 Tons of Stores - Detached 25 C.S.L Tents. Issued stores to units which called. Lent 1 Small Marquee & 1 bell Tent to O.C. Mechanical Transport in town. Lent skids to Batt. Went to Bethune for local purchase purposes & bought 15 Lamps & 20 Red flags & Sticks for A.P.M. Paid for 20 locks & forms ordered previously.	

W Kirmes Capt
D.A.O.M.S 40th Dr

1875   Wt. W593/826   1,000,000   4/15   J.B.C. & A.   A.D.S.S./Forms/C. 2118.

Place	Date	Hour	Summary of Events and Information
Bruay	20/4/16		Issued 3" Trench Mortars (8) to 121st Brigade. Issued 22 Bicycles to R.E. & a large quantity of General Stores. Started Shoemakers Shop & withdrew 7 armourers from Units for Armourers Shop. Went to Chocques (railhead) & selected certain stores returned from Salvage Officer. In afternoon went to Bethune & purchased Muslin. Secured a water cart on loan from the Bonniere.

A.S. Lennie Capt
DADOS 40th Div

WAR DIARY
or
INTELLIGENCE SUMMARY
(Erase heading not required.)

Instructions regarding War Diaries and Intelligence Summaries are contained in F. S. Regs., Part II. and the Staff Manual respectively. Title Pages will be prepared in manuscript.

Army Form C. 2118

Place	Date	Hour	Summary of Events and Information	Remarks and references to Appendices
Bonay	21/6/16		Issued 500 Steel Helmets to 121st Brigade. Sketched 2 tons of General Stores from Railhead. Arranged to hold 100 pairs of Boots to reserve in Shoemakers Shop — remainder there. Motored to Noeux-les-Mines to see D.A.D.O.S. 16 Dvn & ascertained round the position of units of the 46th Dvn who had moved "up". Motored to Railhead & arranged for Thresh Disinfector to be lent from Choques to Bonay at request of A.D.M.S.	
			McInnes Capt D.A.D.O.S 46th Dvn	

1875 Wt. W593/826 1,000,000 4/15 J.B.C. & A. A.D.S.S./Forms/C. 2118.

Place	Date	Hour	Summary of Events and Information	Remarks and references to Appendices
Bomy	22/8/16		Went to Bethune & brought back specimens of Infantry Screens from 15½ Div for inspection of G.O.C. Fetched 3 Tons of General Stores from Railhead. Issued 24 Trench mortars (2") to R.F.A. Reid & practically all the Stores in Dump. Rang up 1st Army & arranged early delivery of 20 Trench Cartons here as usual — 5 Tons of general stores advised & 2000 Steel Helmets	

Andrews Capt
DADOS 48th Divn

WAR DIARY
or
INTELLIGENCE SUMMARY
(Erase heading not required.)

Army Form C. 2118

Instructions regarding War Diaries and Intelligence Summaries are contained in F. S. Regs., Part II. and the Staff Manual respectively. Title Pages will be prepared in manuscript.

Place	Date	Hour	Summary of Events and Information	Remarks and references to Appendices
Busy	23/1/16		Went to Bethune about Infantry screens & to hand estimates. Lent to Merville & fetched 8 French Rifles also went to Chocques (railhead) for stores & carried the same.	
				W S James Capt. D.A.D.O.S 40th Div.

1875 Wt. W593/826 1,000,000 4/15 J.B.C. & A. A.D.S.S./Forms/C. 2118.

Place	Date	Hour	Summary of Events and Information	Remarks and references to Appendices
Bruay	24/6/16		Went to Hdqrs Ind RDA at Bouquemaison took 30 Steel Helmets in car - Afternoon went to Lespagnoy to arrange for manufacture of Infantry screens & placed the order. Sent to railhead for Stores & issued.	

Ind Siènnes Capt
IADOS 48th Divn

WAR DIARY
or
INTELLIGENCE SUMMARY
(Erase heading not required.)

Army Form C. 2118

Instructions regarding War Diaries and Intelligence Summaries are contained in F. S. Regs., Part II. and the Staff Manual respectively. Title Pages will be prepared in manuscript.

Place	Date	Hour	Summary of Events and Information	Remarks and references to Appendices
Bray	25/1/16		Went to La Boussière to see A.D.O.S. afterwards to Noeux-les-Mines for 20 steel Helmets left with D.A.D.O.S 16 Div. Motored to Lapugnoy again about Infantry screens. Called again on A.D.O.S – Arranged for 400 to 500 Steel from La Boussière & 20d / Inch of General Stores.	McSieures Capt DA D.O.S 40th Div

1875 Wt. W593/826 1,000,000 4/15 J.B.C. & A. A.D.S.S./Forms/C. 2118.

Place	Date	Hour	Summary of Events and Information	Remarks and references to Appendices
Bruay	26/6/16		Motored to Chocques (railhead) late headqrs 12 Divn to see about 3 P.B. men & take them over. Took them over. Motored to La Bouvrière & took 70 Steel Helmets for colouring. Brought back 100 & 100 linings to be fitted in armourers shop. 2 Trucks of stores rec'd & issues. Issued 4 French Mortars (3") to 120th Brigade also 6 French Carts. D.D.O.S. & A.D.O.S. came to inspect office & dump.	

AStiennes Capt
DADOS 40th Divn

WAR DIARY
or
INTELLIGENCE SUMMARY
(Erase heading not required.)

Army Form C. 2118

Instructions regarding War Diaries and Intelligence Summaries are contained in F. S. Regs., Part II. and the Staff Manual respectively. Title Pages will be prepared in manuscript.

Place	Date	Hour	Summary of Events and Information	Remarks and references to Appendices
Bruay	27/6/16		Called on A.D.O.S at La Boussière re Supply of Dubbin Demanded 6000 3oz Tins from Base on G.O.C's instructions Motored to Noeux-Les-Mines re Steel Helmets. Failed to get any from D.A.D.O.S's of 16th & 1st Div⁹ Issued from balance of Stock 299 Helmets to 121st Brigade — afternoon motored to Béthune (Local Purchase) Rec⁰. 1 Ton of general Stores including 610 Box Respirators.	

J.M. James Capt.
D.A.D.O.S 40th Div⁹

1875   Wt. W593/826   1,000,000   4/15   J.B.C. & A.   A.D.S.S./Forms/C. 2118.

WAR DIARY
or
INTELLIGENCE SUMMARY
(Erase heading not required.)

Army Form C. 2118

Place	Date	Hour	Summary of Events and Information	Remarks and references to Appendices
Bruay	28/4/16		Motored to Bethune & Noeux-les-Mines & tried to obtain the loan of 4 Tarpaulins for R.F.A. from D.A.D.O.S of 1st & 16th Div⁰ˢ. Failed — Tried Salvage Dump & Stations at Bethune & Noeux — Failed — Obtained a part worn Tarpaulin from D.D.O 1st Corps La Boussière & sent it by Lorry to Ordnance Dump 40th Div⁰. Motored to Douguières to see O.O.C R.F.A also saw O.C. S.A.C. Settled all outstanding questions relating to Mule Charios — Tarpaulins & Rope for Buffers of Guns.	

LaSiennes Capt
D.A.D.O.S 40th Div⁰

| WAR DIARY or INTELLIGENCE SUMMARY | | | Army Form C. 2118 |

WAR DIARY
or
INTELLIGENCE SUMMARY
(Erase heading not required.)

Army Form C. 2118

Instructions regarding War Diaries and Intelligence Summaries are contained in F. S. Regs., Part II. and the Staff Manual respectively. Title Pages will be prepared in manuscript.

Place	Date	Hour	Summary of Events and Information	Remarks and references to Appendices
Bruay	29/6/16		Wired for Lewis Guns 2 per Battalion to Have Motors to Bethune to buy Lamps Hurricane &c Rec? 3 Tons of Stores including 3000 Steel Helmets & 09 Boxes of Box Respirators. Issued almost all the Stores on hand.	

W Gaines Capt
DADOS 40th Div

1875   Wt. W593/826   1,000,000   4/15   J.B.C. & A.   A.D.S.S./Forms/C. 2118.

Place	Date	Hour	Summary of Events and Information	Remarks and references to Appendices
Bruay	30/6/16		Arranged a scheme with AA+QMG & I.O.M. No 24 Workshop – La Bouvrière for mending & strengthening Field Kitchens, G.S. Limbered Wagons & Watercarts without demobilising any unit as to vehicles. Motored to La Bouvrière to see I.O.M. & submit scheme in form of Divisional Order – approved by him. Bought stores in Bethune – Sent all Empty packing Cases ex.e back to Base. Between June 1st & 30th 2,111 Indents have been passed – 84 Bulk Lorries have been despatched & have received & distributed to units 85 Tons of Stores, contained in 24 Trucks. W. Siennes Capt. DADOS 40th Div July 1st 1916	

Headquarters,
40th Division

Herewith the original & one
copy of my War Diary for June 8.

CM Heuves

August 2/16

DADOS 40th Division

Capt.
DADOS 40th Division

WAR DIARY or INTELLIGENCE SUMMARY

Original 40 Leely
40 Div DADOS
Vol 2

Place	Date	Hour	Summary of Events and Information	Remarks and references to Appendices
Bray	July 1st		Rec'd 9 Tons of stores & distributed the greater part of them. Sent motor to Bethune for Lieut Evatt - Inspector of Armourers Shops. Motored to Bethune in afternoon to see I.O.M No 1 Ordnance Workshop about damaged gun belonging to C. Batty 175th Bde. Called on A.A.Q.M.G 1st Corps about repair of vehicles at No 24 Workshop = also called on acting A.D.O.S 1st Corps (Capt Murphy)	

W. Heines Capt
DADOS of 8th Div

WAR DIARY
or
INTELLIGENCE SUMMARY
(Erase heading not required.)

Army Form C. 2118

Instructions regarding War Diaries and Intelligence Summaries are contained in F. S. Regs., Part II. and the Staff Manual respectively. Title Pages will be prepared in manuscript.

Place	Date	Hour	Summary of Events and Information	Remarks and references to Appendices
Bruay	2/7/16		Rec'd 3 Tons of Stores including 800 Steel Helmets & issued these. Went to Bethune in afternoon to see S.I.O. H about 4 faulty guns – Saw Major Truscott & arranged with him to inspect 8 (18 Pr) guns handed over to 40th Div'n by 12th Div'n. Routine work – W Diennes Capt. D.A.D.O.S. 4th Div'n	

1875   Wt. W593/826   1,000,000   4/15   J.B.C. & A.   A.D.S.S./Forms/C. 2118.

Place	Date	Hour	Summary of Events and Information	Remarks and references to Appendices
Bruay	3/7/16		Motored to Lapugnoy about Infantry screens. Went on to Lillers to rehearse scheme for the issue of stores to units in an advance (D.D.O.S.'s scheme, 1st Army). Called at Salvage Dump at Lillers & Chocques & secured steel helmets, Bandoliers, 4 Part worn Tarpaulins & 3 Bundles of old ground sheets, all required forsooie. Routine office work.	

W Deemes Capt
D.A.D.O.S. 40th Div

WAR DIARY
or
INTELLIGENCE SUMMARY
(Erase heading not required.)

Army Form C. 2118

Instructions regarding War Diaries and Intelligence Summaries are contained in F. S. Regs., Part II. and the Staff Manual respectively. Title Pages will be prepared in manuscript.

Place	Date	Hour	Summary of Events and Information	Remarks and references to Appendices
Noeux les Mines	4/7/16		Moved from Bruay to Noeux-les-Mines. Moved 6 Tons of Stores by Lorry — Took over Dump & Workshops of 11th Div?. Found billets and messing accommodation for men consisting of 21 A.O.C. personnel (including 7 armourers) 3 Old Clothes men (P.B's) 2 armourers attached for tests. Settled in — Cleaning &c.	

W Menzies Capt.
D.A.D.O.S 40th Div

1875 Wt. W593/826 1,000,000 4/15 J.B.C. & A. A.D.S.S./Forms/C. 2118.

Place	Date	Hour	Summary of Events and Information	Remarks and references to Appendices
Noeux les Mines	5/7/16		Moved Office & Shoemakers shop over Railway Crossing. Shifted Reserve Stores into old Office (1st Div). Established Armourers in rear of Reserve Store. Secured Benches. Issued Stores. Routine Office Work.	

W J Rennies Capt
D.A.D.O.S 46th Divn

WAR DIARY
or
INTELLIGENCE SUMMARY
(Erase heading not required.)

Army Form C. 2118

Instructions regarding War Diaries and Intelligence Summaries are contained in F. S. Regs., Part II. and the Staff Manual respectively. Title Pages will be prepared in manuscript.

Place	Date	Hour	Summary of Events and Information	Remarks and references to Appendices
Noeux les mines	6/7/16		Rec⁴ 5 Tons of Stores from Base (Oils & Lubricants) Finished armourers Shop – Seventy five Rifles repaired & for issue. Motored to Bethune to No 1. Ordnance Workshop about strengthening Field Kitchens & G.S. Limbered wagons. A.D.D.V.S called & stayed an hour. Issued 3 Tons of stores	
			McBrennie Capt D.A.D.V.S 40th Div	

1875 Wt. W593/826 1,000,000 4/15 J.B.C. & A. A.D.S.S./Forms/C. 2118.

Place	Date	Hour	Summary of Events and Information	Remarks and references to Appendices
Noeux les Mines	7/7/16		Motored to Bethune re repairs to vehicles & inspect a statement I.O.M. No 1. Workshop. Went to Loose No 2 (Coalmine) for 3 scaffold poles (Les Pureles) to support a Tail cover the roof of the armourers Shop - Recd 5 Tons of Stores (General) Issued Same - Visited Salvage Dump - Noeux les Mines W. Hernes Capt D.A.D.O.S 47th Div	

WAR DIARY
or
INTELLIGENCE SUMMARY
(Erase heading not required.)

Army Form C. 2118

Instructions regarding War Diaries and Intelligence Summaries are contained in F. S. Regs., Part II. and the Staff Manual respectively. Title Pages will be prepared in manuscript.

Place	Date	Hour	Summary of Events and Information	Remarks and references to Appendices
Noeux les mines	8/7/16		Rec.d 14 Tons of Stores (chiefly Horse Shoes) Motored to Bethune to Salvage Dump Took an armourers Bench, 100 Steel Helmets 12 Bayonets & scabbards, 100 Pull throughs & oil Bottles &c. &c. Office work on Returns — correspondence &c	
			U.D. Cennies Capt. D.A.D.O.S. 4 8th Di.	

1875   Wt. W593/826   1,000,000   4/15   J.B.C. & A.   A.D.S.S./Forms/C. 2118.

WAR DIARY or INTELLIGENCE SUMMARY

(Erase heading not required.)

Place	Date	Hour	Summary of Events and Information	Remarks and references to Appendices
Noeux les Mines	9/7/16		Rec'd 2 Tons of stores from Base (chiefly clothing) Issued all day & practically cleared. Sent for salvage stores at Bethune. Inspected workshops - Office routine work.	

CW Dennes Capt.
DADOS 47th Div.

WAR DIARY
or
INTELLIGENCE SUMMARY
(Erase heading not required.)

Army Form C. 2118

Instructions regarding War Diaries and Intelligence Summaries are contained in F. S. Regs., Part II. and the Staff Manual respectively. Title Pages will be prepared in manuscript.

Place	Date	Hour	Summary of Events and Information	Remarks and references to Appendices
Noeux les mines	10/7/16		Recᵈ 3 Tons of General Stores (chiefly Picketting (air) Lieut Lankester motored to Lapugnoy to pay for 100 Infantry Screens – Secured a chaff cutter from 1ˢᵗ Corps Troops. Lieut Lankester also called on D.O.1 Corps at La Bourière Motored to Brigade Head qrs at La Brébis saw Staff Capt of 3 Infantry Bdes. Motored to Bethune to Salvage Dump. Brought back 10 Steel Helmets & bespoke 3 Vermorel Sprayers. Issued Stores &c. Office Routine work &c.	

AW Steuner's Capt
D.H.D.O.S.
40ᵗʰ Divⁿ

Place	Date	Hour	Summary of Events and Information	Remarks and references to Appendices
Noeux les Mines	11/7/16		Received 2 Tons of Stores from Base and 150 Stretchers. Went to Salvage Dump at Noeux & Bethune for Vermoral Sprayers & Steel Helmets. Motored in the afternoon to Houchin to Gas Reserve School & Transferred 3 Tents to them from Quartermaster Sergt. of the Camp at that Place. Office Routine work. CW Cienes Capt. D.A.D.O.S. 46th Div.	

WAR DIARY
or
INTELLIGENCE SUMMARY
(Erase heading not required.)

Army Form C. 2118

Instructions regarding War Diaries and Intelligence Summaries are contained in F. S. Regs., Part II. and the Staff Manual respectively. Title Pages will be prepared in manuscript.

Place	Date	Hour	Summary of Events and Information	Remarks and references to Appendices
Noeux les Mines	12/7/16		Recd. 1 Ton of Stores - Issued 229 Helmets Steel Transferred 18 Tents from Tourgnieres to La Bourriere on instructions recd. from 1st Corps. (O.O. Corps 10. D.A.O.S. 16th Dvn 8.) Motored to Bethune in afternoon for Local Purchase - Bought materials etc for Tailors Shop. Visited salvage Dumps in the area for Tarpaulins Camp Kettles & Steel Helmets. W.D. Jeunes Capt. D.A.D.M. 48th Dvn	

1875 Wt. W593/826 1,000,000 4/15 J.B.C. & A. A.D.S.S./Forms/C. 2118.

Place	Date	Hour	Summary of Events and Information	Remarks and references to Appendices
Noeux les Mines	13/7/16		Recd 3 Tons of General Stores - Motored to Headqrs 1st Corps to see A.D.S. re Tents. One Cart Water Tank came up for Div'l purposes as a reserve vehicle - Sent to I.O.M No.1 Workshop Bethune - Went to Bruay to see Town Major & settle up an outstanding matter connected with the payment of the Ordnance Dump lately occupied by the Ordnance of this Division - Proceeded to Chocques to see Pte Cattell A.O.C. & found he had been evacuated to the Base suffering with Rheumatic Fever. Applied for a substitute. A.D.V.S called & spent an hour & a half here.	

C.W. Mesnes Capt
D.A.D.O.S 46th Div

WAR DIARY
or
INTELLIGENCE SUMMARY
(Erase heading not required.)

Army Form C. 2118

Instructions regarding War Diaries and Intelligence Summaries are contained in F. S. Regs., Part II. and the Staff Manual respectively. Title Pages will be prepared in manuscript.

Place	Date	Hour	Summary of Events and Information	Remarks and references to Appendices
Noeux les Mines	14/7/16		Rec⁴. 4 Tons of Stores (chiefly Soap & grease) Lieut Lankester left for the 31st Division - Office work all the morning. Afternoon motored to Marve to inspect a reserve store of 1000 Gas Helmets in that place. Called at Salvage Dump at Le Brebis Visited the Brigades - all apparently satisfied. WD Ceunes Capt D.A.D.V.S. 46th Div⁴	

1875 Wt. W593/826 1,000,000 4/15 J.B.C. & A. A.D.S.S./Forms/C. 2118.

Place	Date	Hour	Summary of Events and Information	Remarks and references to Appendices
Noeux les Mines	15/7/16		Recd 9 Tons of Stores (chiefly Horse Shoes). Morning Office work - Inspection of Shops. Motored during the afternoon to Bethune for Local Purchase. Brassards (yellow) Turkey Twill, aprons, wire, Whitewash Brushes. Issued all stores & dump to clear. W Dieunes Capt D.A.D.V.S 4th Div.	

WAR DIARY
or
INTELLIGENCE SUMMARY
(Erase heading not required.)

Army Form C. 2118

Instructions regarding War Diaries and Intelligence Summaries are contained in F. S. Regs., Part II. and the Staff Manual respectively. Title Pages will be prepared in manuscript.

Place	Date	Hour	Summary of Events and Information	Remarks and references to Appendices
Noeux les mines	16/7/16		Rec⁰ 4 Tons of Stores - (chiefly Clothing) Issued the greater part - Routine office work - Inspection of workshops.	
			[signature] Capt D.A.D.O.S 40th Div.	

1875 Wt. W593/826 1,000,000 4/15 J.B.C. & A. A.D.S.S./Forms/C. 2118.

Place	Date	Hour	Summary of Events and Information	Remarks and references to Appendices
Noeux les Mines	17/8/16		Received 3 Tons of Stores from Base & issued. A.D.O.S. called & spent the morning examining records & inspecting shops – Salvage dumps &c. Recd. 10,500 P.H.G. Helmets – Issued 6000 (approx) Office Routine work – Shops &c.	

A.S. Lewis Capt.
D.A.D.O.S.
48th Divn.

WAR DIARY
or
INTELLIGENCE SUMMARY
(Erase heading not required.)

Army Form C. 2118

Instructions regarding War Diaries and Intelligence Summaries are contained in F. S. Regs., Part II. and the Staff Manual respectively. Title Pages will be prepared in manuscript.

Place	Date	Hour	Summary of Events and Information	Remarks and references to Appendices
Noeux les mines	18/7/16		Recᵈ 1 Ton of Stores & 120 Cases of P.H.G. Helmets Major Smythe D.A.D.O.S to D.D.O.S 1st Army called & inspected system of Bookkeeping – shops &c Afternoon motored to Bethune, Chocques, Lillers & Bruay – Saw Town Major at Lillers about a billeting matter – Saw O.C. No 1 Casualty Clearing Station & obtained 200 old Blankets for dug outs – Purchased two Brassards for Brig Genˡ Campbell Camp & 80 & Nails for Shoemakers Shop.	

Ardiennes Capt
D.A.D.O.S
40ᵗʰ Divⁿ

1875 Wt. W593/826 1,000,000 4/15 J.B.C. & A. A.D.S.S./Forms/C. 2118.

WAR DIARY
or
INTELLIGENCE SUMMARY

Army Form C. 2118

Place	Date	Hour	Summary of Events and Information	Remarks and references to Appendices
Noeux les Mines	19/7/16		Rec'd 2 Tons of Stores - Morning Office Work & Inspection of Shops. Hired a Sewing Machine - Afternoon went to Bethune to buy thread for 800 Bomb Buckets to be made in the Div'l Tailors Shop - Purchased 2 pairs of Tailors scissors. Went to No 3 Casualty Clearing Station & Secured 200 Unserviceable Blankets for Shoe Soles. C W O Lewis Capt D A D O S 6th Div'n	

WAR DIARY
or
INTELLIGENCE SUMMARY
(Erase heading not required.)

Army Form C. 2118

Instructions regarding War Diaries and Intelligence Summaries are contained in F. S. Regs., Part II. and the Staff Manual respectively. Title Pages will be prepared in manuscript.

Place	Date	Hour	Summary of Events and Information	Remarks and references to Appendices
Noeux les Mines	20/7/16		Rec'd 2 Tons of General Stores - A.D.O.S. called & inspected shops etc. Motored in afternoon to Bethune for Local Purchase 13. Red Brassard for G.O.C. - 1 Small Forge for Armourers bought on instructions of A.D.O.S. - Went on to No 1 Casualty Clearing Station & secured 300 Blankets - Went on to Lillers & secured 3 Tarpaulins for R.D.a Head 2no. Office routine. Inspection of Workshops.	

W. Menzies Capt
D.A.D. OS 40th Divn

1875 Wt. W593/826 1,000,000 4/15 J.B.C. & A. A.D.S.S./Forms/C. 2118.

Place	Date	Hour	Summary of Events and Information	Remarks and references to Appendices
Noeux les Mines	21/7/16		Rec'd 5 Tons of General Stores & 2 18 Pr Guns. Motored to Bethune for Local Purchase also to La Boussoire for Cash for Imprest account. Motored to Lapugnoy about transferring 100 Infantry Screens to 8th Div. Afternoon motored to Le Brebis re examination of Gas Helmets. Saw Staff Capt & Bde Majors & found the Bde Staff knew the position of Gas Helmet Reserve at Maroc & Colonne. Office Routine & Inspections. W S Leunies Capt D A D O S 48th Div	

WAR DIARY
or
INTELLIGENCE SUMMARY
(Erase heading not required.)

Army Form C. 2118

Instructions regarding War Diaries and Intelligence Summaries are contained in F. S. Regs., Part II. and the Staff Manual respectively. Title Pages will be prepared in manuscript.

Place	Date	Hour	Summary of Events and Information	Remarks and references to Appendices
Noeux les Mines	22/7/16		Recd. 2 Tons of General Stores also 145 Boxes of Horse Shoes. _Morning_ Motored to La Boussoire & drew 500 francs for Imprest a/c – Went on & drew O O 1st Corps & from thence to La Bouvrière to get sand and paint for painting Helmets. _Afternoon_ motored to Bethune to buy cloth for windows of Hospital (Curtains) also webbing for hospital beds – Acetylene Lamps for Field Ambulances (advance dressing stations). Paid for aprons for R.M.C. Office work and usual inspection of Workshops. AWScennes Capt. D.H.D.D.S 45th Div	

1875   Wt. W593/826   1,000,000   4/15   J.B.C. & A.   A.D.S.S./Forms/C. 2118.

Place	Date	Hour	Summary of Events and Information	Remarks and references to Appendices
Noeux les Mines	23/7/16		Recd. 4 Tons of General Stores (chiefly clothing) Issued the greater part of it — Office work & Workshop supervision.	

WJames Capt.
D.A.D.O.S
48th Divn

WAR DIARY
or
INTELLIGENCE SUMMARY
(Erase heading not required.)

Army Form C. 2118

Instructions regarding War Diaries and Intelligence Summaries are contained in F. S. Regs., Part II. and the Staff Manual respectively. Title Pages will be prepared in manuscript.

Place	Date	Hour	Summary of Events and Information	Remarks and references to Appendices
Noeux les mines	24/7/16		Recd. 4 Tons of Stores. Motored to Le Brébis to Head Qrs 120th 121st & 119th Infantry Bdes arranged for 750 Helmets Ros to go to Loos as a reserve – Part of these to be taken from Maroc & part a fresh issue (additional) Bought 5 acetylene Hurricane Lamps for advance dressing stations. Visited Salvage dumps & secured a good supply of grenade Rifles. Office & Routine Work. Inspection & supervision of shops. W. Sievnes Capt D.A.D.O.S. 45th Div	

1875   Wt. W593/826   1,000,000   4/15   J.B.C. & A.   A.D.S.S./Forms/C. 2118.

WAR DIARY or INTELLIGENCE SUMMARY

Place	Date	Hour	Summary of Events and Information	Remarks and references to Appendices
Noeux les Mines	25/7/16		Received 2 Tons of Stores & Issued. Store cleared. Motored to Bethune in the morning. Local Purchases also to La Boussiere & drew 500 francs for the Imprest account. Afternoon A.D.O.S called & inspected books a/cs etc. C W Dennis Capt D.A.D.O.S 48th Div.	

WAR DIARY
or
INTELLIGENCE SUMMARY
(Erase heading not required.)

Instructions regarding War Diaries and Intelligence Summaries are contained in F. S. Regs., Part II. and the Staff Manual respectively. Title Pages will be prepared in manuscript.

Army Form C. 2118

Place	Date	Hour	Summary of Events and Information	Remarks and references to Appendices

Noeux les Mines	26/7/16		Rec⁴. 1 Ton of Stores and Issued — Store cleared except for small "Stock". Went out most of the day with A.D.O.S on a tour of inspection.
			
			         W² Iennes Capt.
			         D.A.O.V.S 48ᵗʰ Div.	

1875 Wt. W593/826 1,000,000 4/15 J.B.C. & A. A.D.S.S./Forms/C. 2118.

Place	Date	Hour	Summary of Events and Information	Remarks and references to Appendices
Noeux les Mines	27/7/16		Rec'd 1 Ton of Stores and 42 Bicycles. Motored to Le Brébis about Bombing Buckets and Bombing Belts. Brought back a Bombing Shield for alteration in Armourers shop. Motored to Bethune Salvage Dump & Lillers Salvage Dump & obtained a good supply of Grenade rifles. Office Routine o.c. M Diennes Capt DADOS 45th Div	

WAR DIARY
or
INTELLIGENCE SUMMARY
(Erase heading not required.)

Army Form C. 2118

Instructions regarding War Diaries and Intelligence Summaries are contained in F. S. Regs., Part II. and the Staff Manual respectively. Title Pages will be prepared in manuscript.

Place	Date	Hour	Summary of Events and Information	Remarks and references to Appendices
Noeux les Mines	28/7/16		Rec.ᵈ 6 Tons of General Stores & Issued the same — Morning office work & inspection of work in shops. Afternoon 3-30 pm to 5 pm at Bethune for Local Purchase — Sent to Sellers for 5·2 Grenade Rifles — W.J. Leines Capt. D.A.D.O.S 48ᵗʰ Dⁿ	

1875 Wt. W593/826 1,000,000 4/15 J.B.C. & A. A.D.S.S./Forms/C. 2118.

WAR DIARY or INTELLIGENCE SUMMARY

Army Form C. 2118

Place	Date	Hour	Summary of Events and Information	Remarks and references to Appendices
Noeux les Mines	29/7/16		Rec'd 7 Tons of Stores & 42 Bicycles. Issued — Routine work. Morning — afternoon Bethune — Paid for operating aprons and arranged with I.O.M. about repairs to wheels. — W. Mennes Capt. D.A.D.O.S 48th Div	

WAR DIARY
or
INTELLIGENCE SUMMARY

(Erase heading not required.)

Army Form C. 2118

Instructions regarding War Diaries and Intelligence Summaries are contained in F. S. Regs., Part II. and the Staff Manual respectively. Title Pages will be prepared in manuscript.

Place	Date	Hour	Summary of Events and Information	Remarks and references to Appendices
Noeux les mines	30/7/16		Rec⁴ 4 Tons of Stores – (chiefly Clothing) Morning occupied in writing up diary afternoon Motored to Le Brébis & called on all B⁴ᵉ Head q⁺ˢ Staffs. Matter primarily discussed – Bombing Bags – Belts & satchels – Designs submitted & approved to made in Div¹ Tailors & armourers shops. ⟨signature⟩ Capt D.A.D.O.S 48ᵗʰ Div.	

1875 Wt. W593/826 1,000,000 4/15 J.B.C. & A. A.D.S.S./Forms/C. 2118.

Place	Date	Hour	Summary of Events and Information	Remarks and references to Appendices
Noeux les Mines	31/7/16		Rec? 6 Tons of Stores (chiefly Picketting gear) Issued the whole of it. Motored to Bethune for Local Purchase.	

Summary for month of July

No of Indents rec? checked & passed	2478
Tons of Stores received & issued	1644
No of purchases made	39
Amount of money expended sterling } DADOS	£ 59.9/8
No of units purchases authorised	18
amount of money expended sterling }	£ 15 8/2

Divisional Armourers Shop

Rifles overhauled repaired & cleaned	331
Rifles Grenade	360
Bicycles overhauled & repaired	40
Vermorel Sprayers repaired & cleaned	31
Lewis Guns repaired & cleaned	9

Divisional Tailors Shop (3 weeks)

Panties repaired & cleaned №	68
Bombing Bags made	150
Curtains for Field ambulance Hospital	18
Pt Carts repaired	7

Divisional Boot Shop

No rec? & repaired & issued № 825
Average No of men 5½
Average output per man per day 4 8/11
Average No per diem 26 Pairs

Greenies Capt
DADOS 40th Div

WAR DIARY
or
INTELLIGENCE SUMMARY
(Erase heading not required.)

Army Form C. 2118

Instructions regarding War Diaries and Intelligence Summaries are contained in F. S. Regs., Part II. and the Staff Manual respectively. Title Pages will be prepared in manuscript.

Place	Date	Hour	Summary of Events and Information	Remarks and references to Appendices
Noeux les mines	Aug 1st		Rec.? 1 Ton of General Stores (chiefly necessaries) - Issued - Motored to La Boussière for cash for Imprest account also to La Bourière for paint for Steel Helmets Motored to Bethune for Webbing for Field ambulances Cotton & Thread for Tailors shop - Sent 400 tested & 128 untested but new D.H.G Gas Helmets to Maroc for Loos Reserve - Office & Routine work.	

Lt Steiner Capt.
D.A.D.O.S 40th Div.

WAR DIARY or INTELLIGENCE SUMMARY

Place	Date	Hour	Summary of Events and Information	Remarks and references to Appendices
Noeux les Mines	Aug 2nd		Recd 1 Ton of General Stores - Started building Bicycle Shed in Armourers Shop - Took down an old Cook house for this purpose & utilized the material. Office & Routine work &c - Store clear of Stores. W. Steiner Capt D.A.D.O.S. 48th Divn	

WAR DIARY
or
INTELLIGENCE SUMMARY
(Erase heading not required.)

Army Form C. 2118

Instructions regarding War Diaries and Intelligence Summaries are contained in F. S. Regs., Part II. and the Staff Manual respectively. Title Pages will be prepared in manuscript.

Place	Date	Hour	Summary of Events and Information	Remarks and references to Appendices
Noeux les Mines	Aug 3		Rec'd 1 Ton of General Stores – Office Work on Returns Indents &c all day – Inspection of Workshops. W. Pearnes Capt D.H.D.O.S. 40th Div'n	

1875 Wt. W593/826 1,000,000 4/15 J.B.C. & A. A.D.S.S./Forms/C. 2118.

WAR DIARY
or
INTELLIGENCE SUMMARY

Army Form C. 2118

Place	Date	Hour	Summary of Events and Information	Remarks and references to Appendices
Noeux les Mines	Aug 4th		Rec'd 7 Tons of Stores (chiefly Lubricants & Soap) Motored to Bethune for 57 yards of Muslin - Canvas for ambulance stretchers cr.o. - Office work - Inspection of Shops. Afternoon A.D.D.S. 1st Corps called & inspected some vehicles. EWD Lennies Capt. D.A.D.O.S. 40th Divn	

WAR DIARY
or
INTELLIGENCE SUMMARY
(Erase heading not required.)

Army Form C. 2118

Instructions regarding War Diaries and Intelligence Summaries are contained in F. S. Regs., Part II. and the Staff Manual respectively. Title Pages will be prepared in manuscript.

Place	Date	Hour	Summary of Events and Information	Remarks and references to Appendices
Noeux les Mines	Aug 5		Rec⁴ 8 Tons of Stores — Issued these — Motored to Bethune bought acatyline Lamps — Paid for webbing for field Ambᶜᵉˢ (109 metres) Motored to Le Brebis afternoon & visited QMRS Stores in 121ˢᵗ Bde. Found ordnance matters correct. Office & Routine work. Inspection of Shops	

A W Lennes Capᵗ
D. A. D. O. S. 40ᵗʰ Dᵛⁿ

1875 Wt. W593/826 1,000,000 4/15 J.B.C. & A. A.D.S.S./Forms/C. 2118.

WAR DIARY
~~INTELLIGENCE SUMMARY~~

(Erase heading not required.)

Army Form C. 2118

Place	Date	Hour	Summary of Events and Information	Remarks and references to Appendices
Noeux les Mines	Aug 6		Recd 1 Ton of Stores — Inspector of Ordnance & inspected armourers Shops & the work of 3 armourers with the 13th Yorks at Le Brebis — A Lewis Gun arrived for the 19th RWF to replace one unserviceable. Inspected Workshops. Office & general Routine work. W Siennes Capt DADOS. 40th Divn	

WAR DIARY
or
INTELLIGENCE SUMMARY
(Erase heading not required.)

Army Form C. 2118

Instructions regarding War Diaries and Intelligence Summaries are contained in F. S. Regs., Part II. and the Staff Manual respectively. Title Pages will be prepared in manuscript.

Place	Date	Hour	Summary of Events and Information	Remarks and references to Appendices
Noeux les Mines	Aug 7		Rec⁰ 3 Tons of Stores (chiefly picketting gear) motored to Bethune R.E. Workshops for Rods, Cups & Cartridges for Grenade Rifles – also to Mobile Workshop N⁰.1. Bethune thence to Lillers R.O.O. for Rifles – old Tarpaulins & Steel Helmets – Inspection of Workshops – office & routine work.	

W⁰ Leuné? Capt.
D.A.O.O.S. 46ᵗʰ Dₙ.⁴

1875   Wt. W593/826   1,000,000   4/15   J.B.C. & A.   A.D.S.S./Forms/C. 2118.

Place	Date	Hour	Summary of Events and Information	Remarks and references to Appendices
Noeux les Mines	Aug 8		Rec'd 1 Ton of Stores & Issued - all clear. Purchased Buckles for Bomb Belts in Bethune. Inspection of Shops — office routine work. A.W. Siemens Capt. D.A.D.O.S. 47th Div'n	

WAR DIARY
or
INTELLIGENCE SUMMARY
(Erase heading not required.)

Army Form C. 2118

Instructions regarding War Diaries and Intelligence
Summaries are contained in F. S. Regs., Part II.
and the Staff Manual respectively. Title Pages
will be prepared in manuscript.

Place	Date	Hour	Summary of Events and Information	Remarks and references to Appendices
Noeux les Mines	Aug 9		Rec⁴ 1 Ton of Stores — Issued — Inspect⁴ of armourer shops called again Motored to Bethune for local purchase. Inspected Shops — Office routine work. W.S.Menzies Capt. D.A.D.O.S. 48th Div	

1875   Wt. W593/826   1,000,000   4/15   J.B.C. & A.   A.D.S.S./Forms/C. 2118.

WAR DIARY or INTELLIGENCE SUMMARY

Army Form C. 2118

Place	Date	Hour	Summary of Events and Information	Remarks and references to Appendices
Noeux les Mines	Aug 10		Rec'd 1 Ton of Stores — Issued — Morning spent in fixing up New Salvage or Receipt Store. Afternoon motored to Bethune to buy Hurricane Lamps & Muslin — Called at R.E. Depot Mingx for wood. Shop inspection — office & routine work. L. S. Deuues Capt DADOS 46th Div"	

WAR DIARY
or
INTELLIGENCE SUMMARY.
(Erase heading not required.)

Army Form C. 2118.

Instructions regarding War Diaries and Intelligence Summaries are contained in F. S. Regs., Part II. and the Staff Manual respectively. Title pages will be prepared in manuscript.

Place	Date	Hour	Summary of Events and Information	Remarks and references to Appendices
Voeux les mines	Aug 11		Rec⁴ 4 Tons of Stores — all Issued. Motored to La Bouvrière for Sand & Paint for Steel Helmets also to Bouvay for Boots &c. Office & routine work — Inspection of Shops. Ad⁴ienness Capt. D.A.D.O.S. 40th Div⁴	

Place	Date	Hour	Summary of Events and Information	Remarks and references to Appendices
Noeux les Mines	Aug 12th		Rec'd 6 Tons of Stores (chiefly Horse Shoes) Issued. Started new Salvage Shed & took over all Div'l Salvage Stores. Sent 3 G.S. wagons full to Railhead. Ammunition to Lapugnoy. Steel Helmets to La Bouvrière. Office Routine work - Inspection of Shops &c.	

A.B. Levine Capt
DADOS 40th Div'n

WAR DIARY
or
INTELLIGENCE SUMMARY.
(*Erase heading not required.*)

Army Form C. 2118.

Instructions regarding War Diaries and Intelligence Summaries are contained in F. S. Regs., Part II. and the Staff Manual respectively. Title pages will be prepared in manuscript.

Place	Date	Hour	Summary of Events and Information	Remarks and references to Appendices
Noeux les Mines	Aug 13ᵗʰ		Recᵈ 3 Tons of Stores and Issued – Completed Salvage Shed. Office routine Work – Inspection of Workshops etc	
			Clᵒ Siennes Capt DADOS 46ᵗʰ Div	

T2134. Wt. W708—776. 500000. 4/15. Sir J. C. & S.

WAR DIARY or INTELLIGENCE SUMMARY.

Army Form C. 2118.

Place	Date	Hour	Summary of Events and Information	Remarks and references to Appendices
Noeux les Mines	Aug 14th		Recd 3 Tons of Stores (chiefly picketing gear) Motored to Lillers & bought Acetylene Lamps for 119th B⁄d Fetched 2 wagon covers from R.O.O Lillers. Called on ADOS Visited Salvage Dump - Workshops - Old Clothing Store Office routine work &c. W F Iennes Capt. DADOS 40th Dvⁿ	

WAR DIARY
or
INTELLIGENCE SUMMARY.

(Erase heading not required.)

Instructions regarding War Diaries and Intelligence Summaries are contained in F. S. Regs., Part II. and the Staff Manual respectively. Title pages will be prepared in manuscript.

Army Form C. 2118.

Place	Date	Hour	Summary of Events and Information	Remarks and references to Appendices
Noeux les mines	Aug 15		Rec'd 2 Tons of General Stores — Issued. Motored to Bethune for acetylene Lamps & small safety pins for Medal Ribbons — Called at Mirra for missing sections of armstrong Huts. Called at No. 1. Mobile Workshop about manufacture of Mills grenade Extractors. Lent a Lorry load of Ammunition Salved at Houchin to Lapugnoy. Motored to Le T Beits	

T2134.   Wt. W708—776.   500000.   4/15.   Sir J. C. & S.

Place	Date	Hour	Summary of Events and Information	Remarks and references to Appendices
Noeux les Mines	Aug 16		Rec'd 1 Ton of Stores - Issued. Motored to La Boussière, Lillers & Bethune. Bought acetylene Lamps, Hoses etc. Inspected Workshops - Office routine work. W Beames Capt'n DADOS 46th Div	

WAR DIARY
or
INTELLIGENCE SUMMARY.

(Erase heading not required.)

Army Form C. 2118.

Instructions regarding War Diaries and Intelligence Summaries are contained in F. S. Regs., Part II. and the Staff Manual respectively. Title pages will be prepared in manuscript.

Place	Date	Hour	Summary of Events and Information	Remarks and references to Appendices
Naeux les Mines	Aug 17		Rec'd 4 tons of Stores chiefly for Betting gear Grease & oils Issued — Motored to Bethune & bought Stores as per list — Called R.E. workshop for material needed in the armourers shop.	
			W Siennes Capt. D.A.D.O.S. 45th Div	

T2134. Wt. W708—776. 500000. 4/15. Sir J. C. & S.

WAR DIARY
or
INTELLIGENCE SUMMARY.
(Erase heading not required.)

Army Form C. 2118.

Place	Date	Hour	Summary of Events and Information	Remarks and references to Appendices
Noeux les Mines	Aug 18th		Rec'd 4 Tons (General Stores) Issued. Motored to Bethune for specimen of Burns Stove Pricker & other requirements for armourers shops. Office work. Inspection of workshops &c. C W Dennis Capt D.A.O.O. 40th Div	

WAR DIARY
or
INTELLIGENCE SUMMARY.
(*Erase heading not required.*)

Army Form C. 2118.

Instructions regarding War Diaries and Intelligence Summaries are contained in F. S. Regs., Part II. and the Staff Manual respectively. Title pages will be prepared in manuscript.

Place	Date	Hour	Summary of Events and Information	Remarks and references to Appendices
Noeux les Mines	Aug		Recd 4 Tons of Stores – Issued –	
	19th		Motored to Bethune for Bomb from Extractors	
			Band galvanized iron for converted Tins into Buckets	
			Tin clipper – Rivets –	
			Erected Armstrong Hut as a Mess for Tailors	
			Shoemakers &c	
			C. M. Grennie? Capt	
			D.A.D.O.S. 45th Divn	

T2134. Wt. W708—776. 500000. 4/15. Sir J. C. & S.

Place	Date	Hour	Summary of Events and Information	Remarks and references to Appendices
Noeux les Mines	Aug 20th		Rec'd 5 Tons of Stores chiefly Clothing - Office routine work on returns &c all day. A D Reines Capt D A D O S 47th Divn	

WAR DIARY
or
INTELLIGENCE SUMMARY.

(Erase heading not required.)

Army Form C. 2118.

Instructions regarding War Diaries and Intelligence Summaries are contained in F. S. Regs., Part II. and the Staff Manual respectively. Title pages will be prepared in manuscript.

Place	Date	Hour	Summary of Events and Information	Remarks and references to Appendices
Noeux les Mines	Aug 21		Recd 3 Tons of Stores — Chiefly Picketting gear. office routine — Inspected Workshops afternoon motored to Bethune for purchases. CW Seurines Capt D A D O S. 48th Divn	

WAR DIARY or INTELLIGENCE SUMMARY

Army Form C. 2118.

Place	Date	Hour	Summary of Events and Information	Remarks and references to Appendices
Noeux les Mines	Aug		Rec'd 2 Tons of Stores - Issued about 1 15 Prs from ADoS called in morning - Inspection of Workshops &c. Office routine. Motored to Bethune - Chocques - Lillers & Bruay. Secured 150 to 200 Blankets from Casualty Clearing Station at Chocques. also 50 Steel Helmets & 1 Pistol from RDO Lillers - Purchased Khaki cloth at Bruay.	
	22			

C W Lewes Capt
DADOS. 4th Div

WAR DIARY
or
INTELLIGENCE SUMMARY.
(Erase heading not required.)

Army Form C. 2118.

Instructions regarding War Diaries and Intelligence
Summaries are contained in F. S. Regs., Part II.
and the Staff Manual respectively. Title pages
will be prepared in manuscript.

Place	Date	Hour	Summary of Events and Information	Remarks and references to Appendices
Noeux les Mines	Aug 23rd		Rec'd 1 Ton of Stores (Supply General Stores) Issued. Office routine work - Inspection of Workshops morning Afternoon motored to Bethune for purchase of Muslin Observation Kites material &c &c	

CW Ciennes Capt
D.A.D.O.S. 45th Div

T2134. Wt. W708—776. 500000. 4/15. Sir J. C. & S.

WAR DIARY or INTELLIGENCE SUMMARY.

(Erase heading not required.)

Army Form C. 2118.

Place	Date	Hour	Summary of Events and Information	Remarks and references to Appendices
Noeux les Mines	Aug 24th		Recd 2 Tons of Stores - Issued. Motored to see A.D.O.S at La Boussière about Conductor Hilton & Sub Conductor Chadwick who were unwell. Arranged for replacement pending return of these Warrant Officers - Motored on to Lillers to see D.D.O.S 1st Army for confirmation of arrangements. Drew 500 francs for Imprest a/c Motored to La Bouvière. W.D. Jennings Capt D.A.D.O.S. 40th Divn	

WAR DIARY
or
INTELLIGENCE SUMMARY.

(Erase heading not required.)

Instructions regarding War Diaries and Intelligence Summaries are contained in F. S. Regs., Part II. and the Staff Manual respectively. Title pages will be prepared in manuscript.

Army Form C. 2118.

Place	Date	Hour	Summary of Events and Information	Remarks and references to Appendices
Nœux	Aug		Rec⁴ 6 Tons of Stores — Issued.	
les			Routine work in office & Inspection of Shops morning	
Mines	25		afternoon motored to Bethune for purchases & to	
			proceed to See Lieut Proctor Re. re Re. Stores required	
			EW Jennes Capt	
			D A D O S 45ᵗʰ Div	

T2134. Wt. W708—776. 500000. 4/15. Sir J. C. & S.

WAR DIARY
or
INTELLIGENCE SUMMARY.
(Erase heading not required.)

Army Form C. 2118.

Place	Date	Hour	Summary of Events and Information	Remarks and references to Appendices
Noeux	Aug		Rec'd 5 Tons of Stores (chiefly Horseshoes) Issued.	
"			A.D.O.S called & inspected Books in the Office & Workshops	
Mines	26		Obtained 250 Lewis gun magazines from 32nd Division	
			Afternoon motored to Bruay for purchases.	

CwDiennes Capt
D.A.D.O.S 48th Div

WAR DIARY
or
INTELLIGENCE SUMMARY.
(Erase heading not required.)

Army Form C. 2118.

Instructions regarding War Diaries and Intelligence Summaries are contained in F. S. Regs., Part II. and the Staff Manual respectively. Title pages will be prepared in manuscript.

Place	Date	Hour	Summary of Events and Information	Remarks and references to Appendices
Noeux	Aug		Rec⁰ X 2 Tons of Clothing – Issued –	
les			Office routine work – Inspection of workshops	
Mines	27ᵗʰ		morning in Le Brébis with 121ˢᵗ Bde Headqrs	
			Afternoon to La Bouvrière about Steel Helmets	
			W.D. Jennes Capt	
			D.A.D.O.S 46ᵗʰ Divⁿ	

T2134. Wt. W708—776. 500000. 4/15. Sir J. C. & S.

WAR DIARY or INTELLIGENCE SUMMARY.

Army Form C. 2118.

Place	Date	Hour	Summary of Events and Information	Remarks and references to Appendices
Noeux les Mines	Aug 28th		Recd 4 Tons of Stores (General) 1 G.S. Wagon D.H.C Office routine work all day - Inspection of Workshops A. Deviries Capt D.A.D.O.S 40th Div	

WAR DIARY
or
INTELLIGENCE SUMMARY.
(Erase heading not required.)

Army Form C. 2118.

Instructions regarding War Diaries and Intelligence Summaries are contained in F. S. Regs., Part II. and the Staff Manual respectively. Title pages will be prepared in manuscript.

Place	Date	Hour	Summary of Events and Information	Remarks and references to Appendices
Noeux	Aug		Rec'd 2 Tons of Stores (General) Issued.	
les			A.D.O.S 1st Corps with D.D.O.S Lines of Communications (Col Tufnell C.B.)	
Mines	29th		called & spent the morning inspecting & part of the afternoon. Office routine work & inspection of all workshops as usual.	
			C.S. Mennies Capt	
			D.A.D.O.S 4 P.E. Sn	

T2134. Wt. W708—776. 500000. 4/15. Sir J. C. & S.

WAR DIARY or INTELLIGENCE SUMMARY

Army Form C. 2118.

Place	Date	Hour	Summary of Events and Information	Remarks and references to Appendices
Noeux les Mines	Aug 30th		1 Ton of Stores rec'd (Mixed) Issued. Inspection of Workshops — Office routine work. More Magazine arrangements. A.D.O.S called. Afternoon motored to La Bourmière & Bruay. Secured Sand for Helmets — Paint & Brushes & Rivets. WSiennes Capt DADOS 48th Div	

WAR DIARY
or
INTELLIGENCE SUMMARY.
(Erase heading not required.)

Army Form C. 2118.

Instructions regarding War Diaries and Intelligence Summaries are contained in F. S. Regs., Part II. and the Staff Manual respectively. Title pages will be prepared in manuscript.

Place	Date	Hour	Summary of Events and Information	Remarks and references to Appendices
Noeux	Aug		Recd 3 Tons of General Stores — Issued.	
les			Two 18 Pr guns — Morning motored to Le Brebis & visited	
Mines	31st		Bde Headquarters. Office routine work & workshop supervision	
			practically all day	
			C. W. Sleeman Capt	
			O.A.B.O.S. 45th Div	

T2134. Wt. W708—776. 500000. 4/15. Sir J. C. & S.

Place	Date	Hour	Summary of Events and Information	Remarks and references to Appendices
Noeux les Mines	Sept 1st		Rec'd 7 Tons of General Stores - Issued. Also w/d 2 Wagons Limbered G.S. to No 3 Section D.A.C. Motored in morning to Bethune to get White French overcoats Afternoon to La Boussiere & Bruay for purchases also saw A.D.O.S. Office & routine work - Inspection of Workshops. L W Jeunes Capt D.A.D.O.S 40th Divn	

WAR DIARY
or
INTELLIGENCE SUMMARY.
(Erase heading not required.)

Army Form C. 2118.

Instructions regarding War Diaries and Intelligence Summaries are contained in F. S. Regs., Part II. and the Staff Manual respectively. Title pages will be prepared in manuscript.

Place	Date	Hour	Summary of Events and Information	Remarks and references to Appendices
Noeux les mines	Sept	2	Rec⁰ 3 Tons of Horseshoes - Issued. 30 Handcarts arrived for Lewis Guns, also 3 wagons Limbered J.S. N⁰ 2 Section D.A.C. Sent 18 P⁰ Gun to No 1. mobile workshop to replace No 400 condemned. Rec⁰ from mobile workshop 2 3" Stokes guns & 1.2" Trench mortars Inspected workshops - office & routine work. Afternoon went to Lillers & bought Whitewash brushes & 46 also Hammers, Horsechairs & acetylene lamps	

T2134. Wt. W708—776. 500000. 4/15. Sir J. C. & S.

Place	Date	Hour	Summary of Events and Information	Remarks and references to Appendices
Noeux les Mines	Sep 3rd		Rec'd 3 Tons of General Stores (chiefly clothing) also 42 Lewis gun Handcarts - Office routine work Inspection of Workshops Inspection of armourers shop by Lieuts Pratts and Field. CW Siennes Capt D.A.D.O.S 40th Div	

WAR DIARY
or
INTELLIGENCE SUMMARY
(Erase heading not required.)

Army Form C. 2118.

Instructions regarding War Diaries and Intelligence Summaries are contained in F. S. Regs., Part II. and the Staff Manual respectively. Title pages will be prepared in manuscript.

Place	Date	Hour	Summary of Events and Information	Remarks and references to Appendices
Noeux les Mines	Sept 4th		Recd 2 Tons of General Stores & 26 Lewis Guns. Issued these. Motored to Bethune for Hammers. Bought 44 – Went to La Boussière & drew 500 frs for Imprest a/c – office routine – inspection of shops. Afternoon motored to Mines for corrugated iron for Magazine Hut & Zinc 50 Gallon Tank.	

ACVieunes Capt
D.A.D.O.S 40th Divn

T2134.   Wt. W708—776.   500000.   4/15.   Sir J. C. & S.

Place	Date	Hour	Summary of Events and Information	Remarks and references to Appendices
Noeux les Mines	Sept 5th		Rec'd 2 Tons of General Stores - Issued. Morning Office work - Inspection of Workshops afternoon to Bethune for purchases. A.W. Siennes Capt D A D O S. 40th Divn	

WAR DIARY
or
INTELLIGENCE SUMMARY.
(Erase heading not required.)

Army Form C. 2118.

Instructions regarding War Diaries and Intelligence Summaries are contained in F. S. Regs., Part II. and the Staff Manual respectively. Title pages will be prepared in manuscript.

Place	Date	Hour	Summary of Events and Information	Remarks and references to Appendices
Noeux Les Mines	Sept 6th		Recd 1 Ton of General Stores — Issued. Morning Office routine work — Inspection of Shops afternoon to Letters — Bought more white wash brushes and Hammers etc	

A.B. Lennie Capt
D.A.O.O.S. 46th Divn

T2134. Wt. W708—776. 500000. 4/15. Sir J. C. & S.

WAR DIARY or INTELLIGENCE SUMMARY

Army Form C. 2118.

Place	Date	Hour	Summary of Events and Information	Remarks and references to Appendices
Noeux les Mines	Sept 7th		Rec'd 3 Tons of Stores (general) including 1664 Lewis Magazines — office & routine work Inspection & improvement of shops	

McMenies Capt.
D.A.D.O.S 46th Div.

WAR DIARY
or
INTELLIGENCE SUMMARY.

Army Form C. 2118.

Instructions regarding War Diaries and Intelligence Summaries are contained in F. S. Regs., Part II. and the Staff Manual respectively. Title pages will be prepared in manuscript.

(Erase heading not required.)

Place	Date	Hour	Summary of Events and Information	Remarks and references to Appendices
Noeux	Sept		Rec⁰ 7 Tons of Stores & 2300 Blankets — Issued	
Les			Motored to Bethune & Bruay on purchases	
Mines	8th		Bought some Cooks aprons — Whitewash brushes &c	
			Office routine work — Inspection of Workshops.	
			A.B. Lennie Capt.	
			D.A.D.O.S. 46th Div.	

T2134. Wt. W708—776. 500000. 4/15. Sir J. C. & S.

Place	Date	Hour	Summary of Events and Information	Remarks and references to Appendices
Noeux les Mines	Sept 9th		Rec'd 4 Tons of Stores - Issued - All day in office & workshops AB Lennies Capt DADOS. 46th Div'n	

WAR DIARY
or
INTELLIGENCE SUMMARY
(Erase heading not required.)

Army Form C. 2118.

Instructions regarding War Diaries and Intelligence Summaries are contained in F. S. Regs., Part II. and the Staff Manual respectively. Title pages will be prepared in manuscript.

Place	Date	Hour	Summary of Events and Information	Remarks and references to Appendices
Noeux Les mines	Sp 10th		Rec⁰ 2 Tons of General Stores (chiefly clothing) all day office routine & workshops.	

C.H. Stevens Capt
D.A.D.O.S 40th Div.

T2134. Wt. W708—776. 500000. 4/15. Sir J. C. & S.

Place	Date	Hour	Summary of Events and Information	Remarks and references to Appendices
Noeux les Mines	Sept 11th		Recd 4 Tons of Stores - This includes 1 18 Pr for B. Battery 181st Bde - Morning office & routine work - Inspection of workshops &c. Went to Le Brébis (Bde Head Qrs) about issue of Blankets for 200 men going to sea side afternoon to Lillers for purchases. C.W. Beemes Capt D.A.D.O.S. 40th Div	

WAR DIARY
or
INTELLIGENCE SUMMARY.
(Erase heading not required.)

Army Form C. 2118.

Instructions regarding War Diaries and Intelligence Summaries are contained in F. S. Regs., Part II. and the Staff Manual respectively. Title pages will be prepared in manuscript.

Place	Date	Hour	Summary of Events and Information	Remarks and references to Appendices
Noeux les mines	Sep¹ 12ᵗʰ		Rec⁴ 2 Tons of Stores – also 2020 Blankets Office & routine work. – Inspection of Shops afternoon to La Bourière to see A.D.O.S & afterwards to Bethune for purchases. CW Rennie's Capt D.A.D.O.S 48ᵗʰ Div	

T2134. Wt. W708—776. 500000. 4/15. Sir J. C. & S.

WAR DIARY
or
INTELLIGENCE SUMMARY.
(Erase heading not required.)

Army Form C. 2118.

Instructions regarding War Diaries and Intelligence Summaries are contained in F. S. Regs., Part II. and the Staff Manual respectively. Title pages will be prepared in manuscript.

Place	Date	Hour	Summary of Events and Information	Remarks and references to Appendices
Noeux les Mines	Sept. 13th		Rec'd 1 Ton of General Stores also 2700 Blankets Office routine & inspection of workshops. afternoon to Bethune to buy String & on to Merville for Thornton Horn Cylinders - Lillers for Brassards &c. C.W. Viennes Capt D.A.D. O.S. 40th Div.	

WAR DIARY
or
INTELLIGENCE SUMMARY.
(Erase heading not required.)

Army Form C. 2118.

Instructions regarding War Diaries and Intelligence Summaries are contained in F. S. Regs., Part II. and the Staff Manual respectively. Title pages will be prepared in manuscript.

Place	Date	Hour	Summary of Events and Information	Remarks and references to Appendices
Noeux les Mines	Sep. 14th		Rec'd 2 Tons of General Stores — Issued — also rec'd 255 Cases of Gum Boots — Morning office & Routine work — Inspection of Workshops Motored to La Boursière & Bethune for things for straw mattresses — afternoon to Lillers for Atoms Torches CW Jenkins Capt D.A.D.O.S 40th Div	

T2134. Wt. W708—776. 500000. 4/15. Sir J. C. & S.

Place	Date	Hour	Summary of Events and Information	Remarks and references to Appendices
Noeux les Mines	Sept 15th		Recd. 5 Tons General Stores also 1 wagon S.D. for 4 Section D.A.C. - Recd. 2500 Blankets & 72 Cases of Gum Boots Thigh - also 35 Sacks of Field Boots. Morning office & routine work & inspection of Shops. Afternoon to Bethune for purchase of things for Straw Mattresses & Iron mongery materials for Armourers shop. - La Boussiere for money for Imprest a/c. A.W. Deunis Capt D.A.D.O.S. 46th Divn	

WAR DIARY
or
INTELLIGENCE SUMMARY.
(Erase heading not required.)

Army Form C. 2118.

Instructions regarding War Diaries and Intelligence Summaries are contained in F. S. Regs., Part II. and the Staff Manual respectively. Title pages will be prepared in manuscript.

Place	Date	Hour	Summary of Events and Information	Remarks and references to Appendices
Noeux	Sep^t		Rec^d. 7 Tons of Stores (chiefly Horseshoes)	
les			also 2100 Blankets also 20 Lewis Gun Carts	
mines	16th		All day office routine work & workshops.	
			CWBrennes Capt	
			D A D O S. 40th Div^n	

T2134. Wt. W708—776. 500000. 4/15. Sir J. C. & S.

Place	Date	Hour	Summary of Events and Information	Remarks and references to Appendices
Noeux Les Mines	Sept 17th		Rec'd 3 Tons of General Stores (chiefly clothing) Issued. Also 2000 Blankets & 52 Lewis Gun Handcarts. All issued. Morning office routine & Inspection of Workshops. Afternoon motored to La Boissiere to see A.D.O.S. Audiennes Capt. D.A.D.O.S 46th Div.	

WAR DIARY
or
INTELLIGENCE SUMMARY.

(Erase heading not required.)

Army Form C. 2118.

Instructions regarding War Diaries and Intelligence Summaries are contained in F. S. Regs., Part II. and the Staff Manual respectively. Title pages will be prepared in manuscript.

Place	Date	Hour	Summary of Events and Information	Remarks and references to Appendices
Noeux les Mines	Sept 18th		Rec'd 3 tons of General Stores: issued. Also 2 wagons limbered G.S. for 2 Sect D.A.C. & 1 for 3 Sect D.A.C., also 2260 blankets. Inspected Store & workshops with Capt Renner D.A.D.O.S. who handed over the books etc to me in the evening.	

signature Lieut

for D.A.D.O.S. 40th Div

T2134. Wt. W708—776. 500000. 4/15. Sir J. C. & S.

WAR DIARY or INTELLIGENCE SUMMARY.

Army Form C. 2118.

Place	Date	Hour	Summary of Events and Information	Remarks and references to Appendices
Noeux les Mines	Sept 19th		Rec'd truck of 2 tons General Stores, issued. Also 2120 Blankets. Inspected Old Clothing Store. Office and Routine work. Elliott Selby Lieut for D.A.D.O.S. 47th Div.	

WAR DIARY
or
INTELLIGENCE SUMMARY.

(Erase heading not required.)

Army Form C. 2118.

Instructions regarding War Diaries and Intelligence Summaries are contained in F. S. Regs., Part II. and the Staff Manual respectively. Title pages will be prepared in manuscript.

Place	Date	Hour	Summary of Events and Information	Remarks and references to Appendices
Noeux les Mines.	Sept 20		Received 1 ton of General Stores and 17 Wheels. Inspected Ammunition Dump, and visited Stores and Workshops. Drew frs 500. for Imprest Account from Field Cashier. 6 Corps. Went to Bethune and Lillers for local purchases. D/Comdr Simpson left for 8th Div.	

Edmund Selby Lieut for D.A.D.O.S. 40th Div.

T2134. Wt. W708—776. 500000. 4/15. Sir J. C. & S.

WAR DIARY
INTELLIGENCE SUMMARY.
(Erase heading not required.)

Army Form C. 2118.

Place	Date	Hour	Summary of Events and Information	Remarks and references to Appendices
Noeux les Mines	Sept 21		Received 3 tons of General Stores; issued. Motored to Bethune in morning for local purchases. Saw acting ADOS I Corps. In afternoon visited Railhead. Inspected workshops and Salvage Dump. Received 1319 Boots Gum Thigh from 3rd Divn. Office & Routine work.	

Arnold Selby
Lieut.
a/D.A.D.O.S. 40th Divn.

WAR DIARY
or
INTELLIGENCE SUMMARY.

Army Form C. 2118.

Instructions regarding War Diaries and Intelligence Summaries are contained in F. S. Regs., Part II. and the Staff Manual respectively. Title pages will be prepared in manuscript.

(Erase heading not required.)

Place	Date	Hour	Summary of Events and Information	Remarks and references to Appendices
Noeux les Mines	Sept 22		Received 3 tons of General Stores : issued. Motored to Mazingarbe in morning re Petrol cans. In afternoon motored to Lillers for local purchase. also visited OC Divisional Gas School at Konchin Office & ~~work~~ routine work: inspection of workshops.	
			Ernest Selby Lieut a/Director 46th Div.	

T2134. Wt. W708—776. 500000. 4/15. Sir J. C. & S.

Place	Date	Hour	Summary of Events and Information	Remarks and references to Appendices
Noeux les Mines	Sep. 23rd		Received 5 Tons of General Stores Horseshoes Etc — Issued. — Lieut: E.A. Selby left 40th Division for duty with 49th Div: —	R.A.Hilton Condr: A.V.C. a/D.A.D.O.S. 40th Div=

WAR DIARY
or
INTELLIGENCE SUMMARY.

(Erase heading not required.)

Army Form C. 2118.

Instructions regarding War Diaries and Intelligence Summaries are contained in F. S. Regs., Part II. and the Staff Manual respectively. Title pages will be prepared in manuscript.

Place	Date	Hour	Summary of Events and Information	Remarks and references to Appendices
Noeux les mines	Ap. 24th		Received 8 Tons General stores clothing Etc. Issued. —	
				R.A. Hilton. Condr. A.V.C. O/D. areas 40th Divn

T2134. Wt. W708—776. 500000. 4/15. Sir J. C. & S.

WAR DIARY
or
INTELLIGENCE SUMMARY.

Place	Date	Hour	Summary of Events and Information	Remarks and references to Appendices
Noeux les Mines	Sep. 25th		6 Tons of stores received - Picketting gear Etc.	

R.A. Bilton, Comdg
a/ Dates.
40th Div.

WAR DIARY
or
INTELLIGENCE SUMMARY.

Army Form C. 2118.

Instructions regarding War Diaries and Intelligence Summaries are contained in F. S. Regs., Part II. and the Staff Manual respectively. Title pages will be prepared in manuscript.

(*Erase heading not required.*)

Place	Date	Hour	Summary of Events and Information	Remarks and references to Appendices
Noeux les mines	Sept 26th		1 Ton of General Stores received and issued. Boots Etc.	
				R.A. Milton. Comd: a/c o/c 40th bn:

T2134. Wt. W708—776. 500000. 4/15. Sir J. C. & S.

Place	Date	Hour	Summary of Events and Information	Remarks and references to Appendices
Noeux les mines	Sep 27th		3 tons of general stores received and issued Socks Etc.	

R A Hilton
Conds:
a/b a oo
4 o R bn:

WAR DIARY
or
INTELLIGENCE SUMMARY.
(Erase heading not required.)

Army Form C. 2118.

Instructions regarding War Diaries and Intelligence Summaries are contained in F. S. Regs., Part II. and the Staff Manual respectively. Title pages will be prepared in manuscript.

Place	Date	Hour	Summary of Events and Information	Remarks and references to Appendices
Noeux les mines	Sep. 28th		1 Ton general stores received and issued. Boots and detail. — 3 Aeroplane sheets manufactured in Tailors shops and issued to Hd; Qrs: 40th Divn: —	
			R. A. Hilton. Condr. of Leaves. 40th Divn	

T2134. Wt. W708—776. 500000. 4/15. Sir J. C. & S.

Place	Date	Hour	Summary of Events and Information	Remarks and references to Appendices
Noeux les mines	Sept 29th		4 Tons of stores received and issued - Grease, Soda, & Soap. -	

R.A. Kilton.
Condr: A.O.C.
a/ D.A.D.O.S.
40th Divn

WAR DIARY
or
INTELLIGENCE SUMMARY.
(Erase heading not required.)

Army Form C. 2118.

Instructions regarding War Diaries and Intelligence Summaries are contained in F. S. Regs., Part II. and the Staff Manual respectively. Title pages will be prepared in manuscript.

Place	Date	Hour	Summary of Events and Information	Remarks and references to Appendices
Noeux les mines	Sep. 30th		4 Tons general stores Horseshoes Etc received and Issued — Purchased 5 yards of Wire Gauze for Sanitary Section —	

R.A.Bilton.
Comdr: A.O.C.
a/c. A.D.O.S.
40th Divn

WAR DIARY or INTELLIGENCE SUMMARY.

DADOS Vol 5

Place	Date	Hour	Summary of Events and Information	Remarks and references to Appendices
Noeux les Mines	1916 Oct: 1st		1 Ton general stores and 6 Tons of clothing received and issued. — A.D.O.S. 1st Corps Inspected the Office, Stores and Workshops. —	
	2nd		3 Tons general stores received and issued also 214 bales of clothing Woollen Vests Etc: — Lieut: Geo: Edwardes Lawrence joined Div⁼	
	~~3rd~~		~~1 Ton general stores received and issued~~ R.H. R.A. Wilton. Condr: A.O.C. of orders. 40th Div⁼	
	3rd		The duties of D.A.D.O.S were taken over by me, Geo Edwardes-Lawrence Lieut. A.O.D. One Ton of General Stores were received and Issued.	G.87.H.
	4th		Three tons of general stores received and issued - Cricketing gear etc. D.D.O.S. 1st Army made an inspection of the records kept in the Office, and visited the Workshops and Stores. Geo Edwardes-Lawrence Lieut DADOS 40th Division	

WAR DIARY
or
INTELLIGENCE SUMMARY.
(Erase heading not required.)

Army Form C. 2118.

Instructions regarding War Diaries and Intelligence Summaries are contained in F. S. Regs., Part II. and the Staff Manual respectively. Title pages will be prepared in manuscript.

Place	Date 1916	Hour	Summary of Events and Information	Remarks and references to Appendices
Neuve Eglise	Oct 5"		Six pans of Ferruns stores received and issued - Leeds Warren, Jam co, ration etc.	48.R
to Nunes		6"	Ten pans of Ferruns stores received and issued - Accessories etc, also 11 Wheels for 4.5" Mortar (No 128) and 12 Cords-land Machine Gun.	48.R
		7"	Three pans of Ferruns stores received and issued - Stores incl. 284 etc.	48.R
		8"	One pan of Hares stores received and issued	48.R
		9"	Eight pans of Ferruns stores received and issued	48.R
			Rec'd the Heavy Mobile A.A. Workshop to assist in the salvaging of this area and the light mobile shop to assist in the salvaging of Hill 63Route.	48.R
		10"	One pan of Ferruns stores received and issued	48.R
		11"	Three pans of Ferruns stores received and issued - Clothing etc.	48.R
		12"	Four pans of Ferruns stores received and issued - Hares stores etc.	48.R
		13"	Eight pans of Ferruns stores received and issued - Clothing etc also	48.R
			4.30 alps. Montreuil.	48.R

Lee Edwards Lieuten
Field A & F No 2 Division

T2134. Wt. W708—776. 500000. 4/15. Sh. J.C. & S.

WAR DIARY or INTELLIGENCE SUMMARY.

(Erase heading not required.)

Army Form C. 2118.

Place	Date	Hour	Summary of Events and Information	Remarks and references to Appendices
Noeux les Mines	1916 Oct 14th		Three tons of General Stores received and issued – Boots, Caps &c.	G.84.Lt
	15th		Two tons of General Stores received and issued – Necessaries &c.	G.84.Lt
	16th		Two tons of General Stores received and issued – Grease, Oil &c. Also 200 cases of box respirators.	G.84.Lt
	17th		Two tons of General Stores received and issued – Horseshoes &c.	G.84.Lt
	18th		Five tons of General Stores received and issued – Clothing &c. Also 1 Water Cart.	G.84.Lt
	19th		Four tons of General Stores received and issued – Picketting Gear &c. A conference of Quartermasters, under the direction of DADOS was held at the Mine Buildings Les Brebis.	G.84.Lt
	20th		No Stores arrived.	
	21st		Two tons of General Stores, six tons of Clothing, 200 cases of box respirators, and 240 Rugs horse received and issued.	G.84.Lt G.84.Lt G.84.Lt
	22nd		Four tons of General Stores & 3 Carts water received and issued.	G.84.Lt
	23rd		3,023 Rugs horse received and issued.	G.84.Lt

Geo Edwardes-Lawrence
Lieut. DADOS 40th Division

WAR DIARY
or
INTELLIGENCE SUMMARY.

Army Form C. 2118.

Place	Date	Hour	Summary of Events and Information	Remarks and references to Appendices
Meaulte	1916 24th		One of Junior obs received and round - Fred and Maxime - also 2 Cards of per Large Junior Complete and 140 Cross of per recipients.	23/4/16
La Neuville	25th		Two and 3 Junior obs received and round - Junior Cards etc.	23/4/16
	26th		Also 2 Cards of per recipients.	23/4/16
	27th		One and 3 Junior obs received and round Cards etc. also 3 recipients	23/4/16
	28th		8.77 Grip have received and occupied (the Junior ferry Limited) and 2 Cards taken. in the above) 333 Junior Junior forwarded to the manufacture of ammunition carried by 4. 5. Aero Balloons	23/4/16
	29th		Eastern Aero Beach & mist.	23/4/16
	30th		Left Meaux for Amis and Ferris at Fresilcourt	23/4/16
Bellevue	31st		Arrived Bellevue & Class for Machine Gun Junior Infantry repairs.	23/4/16

La Neuville-Farmin
Field 28.2.5

H.E. Junior

WAR DIARY or INTELLIGENCE SUMMARY

Original
DADOS 40D
Vol X 6
Army Form C. 2118.

Place	Date	Hour	Summary of Events and Information	Remarks and references to Appendices
	1916 Nov			
Roellecourt	1st & 2nd		No Stores received	
	3rd		50 Pairs of Boots received from St Pol Railhead & Issued.	
Frohen le Grand	4th		Left Roellecourt and arrived at Frohen le Grand. Railhead Conteville.	
Berneville	5th		Left Frohen le Grand and arrived at Berneville. Opened Divisional Armourers & Shoemakers Shops. Complaints received about Boots, wired for 1,200 Pairs.	
Berneville	6th		3 Trucks of detail Stores (30 Tons) 1 Watercart and 1 Limbered Wagon received and Issued.	
Berneville	7th		One 3" Stokes Gun received and Issued to 120th T.M.B. also 1 Truck of General Stores (8 Tons) and 5 Trucks containing Winter Clothing and Boots (25 Tons) Boots and 2 Trucks of Fur Coats cleared and issued Jerkins reconsigned.	
Berneville	8th		2 Trucks containing Boots, Cardigans & Vests (12 Tons) received and Issued.	
do	9th		1 Truck containing Dubbin, Oil, Horseshoes &c received and Issued	
do	10th		1 Truck containing Boots F.S. and Gloves fingerless (5 Tons) received and Issued	

Geo Edwardes-Kerens
Lieut DADOS 40th Division.

WAR DIARY
or
INTELLIGENCE SUMMARY.

(Erase heading not required.)

Army Form C. 2118.

August

Place	Date	Hour	Summary of Events and Information	Remarks and references to Appendices
	1916 May			
Beaumont	11ᵗʰ		No stores moved	
do	12ᵗʰ		1 Lorry containing 105 Cases Box Respirators received.	
do	13ᵗʰ		1 Lorry containing three pairs, 10 bales of Respirators and 30 cases etc Helmets received & issued (7 vans).	
do	14ᵗʰ		2 Lorries containing Koeti Jerims, delivery helmets, bales of supplies to complete the 120ᵗʰ Inf. Brigade and the Italian contingent to new Brigade at Beaumesnil.	
Beaumont	15ᵗʰ		Left Beaumont and returned to Italian & hand.	
Intéressant	16ᵗʰ		1 Lorry containing Bask'nits and Jerseys (6 vans) received and issued	
do	17ᵗʰ		30 vans of Cards, drawers and socks received and sent round to Units as required. Pro Clean dump.	
do	18ᵗʰ		Left Intéressant for Beaumesnil. — One lorry loaded received the barkshofs Bathing Sa 14¼" Outfit 7 pair of Helmets.	
Beaumesnil	19ᵗʰ		1 Lorry of Jersey shoes issued and sent (8 vans)	
do	20ᵗʰ		1 Lorry containing shoes-pans, Jaces de received and issued (5 vans)	

No Chrouter Jerseys
Issued 84,285
140½ Dozens

WAR DIARY or INTELLIGENCE SUMMARY

Army Form C. 2118.

Original

Place	Date	Hour	Summary of Events and Information	Remarks and references to Appendices
Bouquemaison	1916 Nov 20th		New underclothing issued and dirty clothing received and disinfected.	
do	21st		Cleared Truck No 23,255 containing D.A.D.O.S. Stores and loaded Stores for dispatch to new Railhead viz Vignacourt.	
do	22nd		Finished loading Stores for Vignacourt.	
do			Left Bouquemaison for Doullens. On arrival at Doullens sent Lorry with Boots for issue to 120th Infy Bde.	
Doullens	23rd		Left Doullens and visited Vignacourt Railhead returned and opened Office at Canaples.	
Canaples	24th		Left Canaples for Ailly le Haut Clocher. Stores cleared from Railhead and Issued to Units commenced.	
Ailly le Haut Clocher	25th		Opened Bootmakers, Armourers and Tailors Shops. 3 Trucks of Stores, Goggles, Respirators, Wheels and General Stores (15 Tons) Cleared and Issued.	
do	26th		1 Truck of Clothing received and Issued (4 Tons.)	
do	27th		1 Truck containing Boots and bulk stores received and Issued (6 Tons).	

Geo Edwards Lawrence
Lieut D.A.D.O.S
40th Division

Army Form C. 2118.

WAR DIARY
or
INTELLIGENCE SUMMARY.

(Erase heading not required.)

Instructions regarding War Diaries and Intelligence Summaries are contained in F. S. Regs., Part II. and the Staff Manual respectively. Title pages will be prepared in manuscript.

Place	Date	Hour	Summary of Events and Information	Remarks and references to Appendices
Achiele { Heart Cheshir {	1916 28" 29" 30"		1 Tunk of Buck Space covered and issued (5 tons) 2 Tunks Cedarwood Buck and Spruce covered and issued (12 tons) 1 Tunk Cedarwood timber, Haverefaces, K.6 and Britten covered and issued (6 tons.) For Exeunto-Foureau Field 9/9/97 40" Division	

T2134. Wt. W708—776. 500000. 4/15. Sr. J. C. & S.

WAR DIARY or INTELLIGENCE SUMMARY

Army Form C. 2118.

Original
DADOS 40D
Vol 7

Place	Date	Hour	Summary of Events and Information	Remarks and references to Appendices
	1916			
Ailly le Haut Clocher	1st Dec		Received and Issued 877 Rugs horse.	
	2nd		Received and Issued 5 Tons of General Stores.	
	3rd		do — do 6 " do do	
"	4th		do do 10 " do do	
"	5th		do do 13 " Boots & Underclothing.	
"	6th		do do 8 " General Stores	
"	7th		do do 12 " do	
"	8th		do do 7 " Clothing	
"	9th		do do 8 " General Stores	
"	10th		do do 6 " do	
"	11th		do do No Stores received this day.	
"	12th		do do — do — do —	
"	13th		do do 5 Tons General Stores.	
"	14th		do do No Stores received this day.	
"	15th		Left Ailly le Haut Clocker for Chipilly	

ho Edwardes Jansenes
Captain DADOS
40th Division

WAR DIARY
or
INTELLIGENCE SUMMARY.
(Erase heading not required.)

Instructions regarding War Diaries and Intelligence Summaries are contained in F. S. Regs., Part II. and the Staff Manual respectively. Title pages will be prepared in manuscript.

Original

Army Form C. 2118.

Place	Date	Hour	Summary of Events and Information	Remarks and references to Appendices
	1916 Dec			
Chipilly	16th		Received and Issued 8 Tons of Stores including 7 Chest of Rifles.	
"	17th		do — do 6 " " Underclothing.	
"	18th		do 7 " " Stores including 1000 Blankets and 4 Chaff Cutters.	
"	19th		do do 8 " " do	
"	20th		do do 5 " " General Stores.	
"	21st		do do No Stores received this day.	
"	22nd		do do do do	
"	23rd		do do 4 Tons General Stores	
"	24th		do do No Stores received this day.	
"	25th		do do 11 Tons General Stores.	
"	26th		do do 8 " do	
"	27th		do do No Stores received this day.	
"	28th		Left Chipilly for Bray Sur Somme	
Bray Sur Somme	"		Received 4 Tons of Stores including 480 Boxes in Magazine Carriers	
	29th		do 5 " do	
			Ho Edwards Lieutenant Captain DADOS 40th Division	

T2134. Wt. W708—776. 500000. 4/15. Sir J. C. & S.

WAR DIARY or **INTELLIGENCE SUMMARY.** *Original*

Army Form C. 2118.

Place	Date	Hour	Summary of Events and Information	Remarks and references to Appendices
Bray sur Somme	1916 Dec 30th		Received and Issued 4 Tons of Stores, Horseshoes, Soap & Grease.	
	31st		No Stores received this day.	

Geo Edwards Lawrence
Captain
DADOS
40th Division.

WAR DIARY
or
INTELLIGENCE SUMMARY.
(Erase heading not required.)

Instructions regarding War Diaries and Intelligence Summaries are contained in F. S. Regs., Part II. and the Staff Manual respectively. Title pages will be prepared in manuscript.

Original
DADOS 40 D
Vol 8

Army Form C. 2118.

Place	Date	Hour	Summary of Events and Information	Remarks and references to Appendices
	1917			
Bray Sur Somme	Jan 1		26 Lewis Guns received and issued to Infantry Battalions. Completed to 12 per Battalion.	
	2nd		18 Tons of Stores received and Issued.	
"	3rd		6 " do do do	
"	4 & 5		No Stores received this day.	
"	6th		8 Tons of Stores received and Issued.	
"	7th		6 " do do do	
"	8th		7 " do do do	
"	9th		10 " do do do	
"	10th		9 " do do do	
"	11th		12 " do do do	
"	12th		8 " do do do	
"	13th		7 " do do do	
"	14th		14 " do do do	
"	15th		8 " do do do	
"	16th		20 " do do do	

Geo Edwardes-Lawrence
Captain DADOS 40th Division

T2134. Wt. W708—776. 500000. 4/15. Sir J. C. & S.

WAR DIARY or INTELLIGENCE SUMMARY.

Army Form C. 2118.

Place	Date	Hour	Summary of Events and Information	Remarks and references to Appendices
Bray sur Somme	1917 Jan 17/18		No Stores received.	
"	19th		8 Tons of Stores received and issued.	
"	20th		5 " do do do	
"	21st		7 " do do do	
"	22nd		9 " do do do	
"	23rd		7 " do do do	
"	24th		6 " do do do	
"	25th		9 " do do do	
"	26th		7 " do do do	
"	27th		No stores received left Bray and opened at Chipilly.	
Chipilly	28th		8 Tons of Stores received and issued	
"	29th		12 " do do do	
"	30th		3 " do do do	

Geo Edwardes-Lawrence
Captain
DADOS
40th Division

WAR DIARY
or
INTELLIGENCE SUMMARY.

Original

(Erase heading not required.)

Army Form C. 2118.

Instructions regarding War Diaries and Intelligence Summaries are contained in F. S. Regs., Part II. and the Staff Manual respectively. Title pages will be prepared in manuscript.

Place	Date	Hour	Summary of Events and Information	Remarks and references to Appendices
Chipilly.	31/7.		Took over the Duties of the L.A.L.O.S. who has proceeded on Leave today. No stores received. — R.A.Hilton. Condr: A.O.C. of L.A.L.O.S. 40th Div.	

T2134. Wt. W708—776. 500000. 4/15. Sir J. C. & S.

WAR DIARY or INTELLIGENCE SUMMARY

Army Form C. 2118.

DADOS 40D Vol 9

Place	Date	Hour	Summary of Events and Information	Remarks and references to Appendices
Chipilly	1/2/17		6 Tons General Stores received and issued —	
	1/2/17			R.A.Wilton. Condr: A.O.C. o/p. a.D.O.S. 40th Divn:
Chipilly	2/2/17		No Truck arrived —	
	2/2/17			R.A.Wilton. Condr: A.O.C. o/p. a.D.O.S. 40th Divn:
Chipilly	3/2/17		5 Tons of Stores bulk Clothing etc received and issued	
	3/2/17			R.A.Wilton. Condr: A.O.C. o/p. a.D.O.S. 40th Divn:
Chipilly	4/2/17		No Truck arrived —	
	4/2/17			R.A.Wilton. Condr: A.O.C. o/p. a.D.O.S. 40th Divn:

WAR DIARY
or
INTELLIGENCE SUMMARY.

(Erase heading not required.)

Army Form C. 2118.

Instructions regarding War Diaries and Intelligence
Summaries are contained in F.S. Regs., Part II.
and the Staff Manual respectively. Title pages
will be prepared in manuscript.

Place	Date	Hour	Summary of Events and Information	Remarks and references to Appendices
Arkville	5/2/17		No trucks arrived –	
			5/2/17.	Ration Cards A.S.C. a/a a.a.o.s. 140 other.
Arkville	6/2/17		No trucks arrived.	
			6/2/17.	Ration Cards A.S.C. a/a a.a.o.s. 140 other.
Arkville	7/2/17		14 tons Junior and bulk stores including fodder.	
			7/2/17.	
Arkville	8/2/17		10 tons bulk and junior stores etc.	
			8/2/17.	ditto
Arkville	9/2/17		No trucks arrived. –	
			9/2/17.	Ration Cards A.S.C. a/a a.a.o.s. 140 other.

2353 Wt W25544/1454 700,000 5/15 D.&L. A.D.S.S. Forms/C 2115.

WAR DIARY or INTELLIGENCE SUMMARY.

Army Form C. 2118.

Instructions regarding War Diaries and Intelligence Summaries are contained in F. S. Regs., Part II. and the Staff Manual respectively. Title pages will be prepared in manuscript.

(Erase heading not required.)

Place	Date	Hour	Summary of Events and Information	Remarks and references to Appendices
Chipilly	10/2/17		6 Tons General Stores received and issued —	
	10/2/17			
Chipilly	11/2/17		No Truck arrived. — Moved from Chipilly to Bray — D.A.D.O.S. returned off leave. —	R.A.Sitton. Condr: a.v.c a/p.a.D.O.S. 40th Divⁿ
Bray sur Somme	1917 Feb 11/2/17			
	12th		4 Tons Equipment etc received and issued	
	13th		8 " Boots, Caps, Socks etc do do	
	14th		61 Rugs horse do do	
	15th		10 Tons General Stores do do	
	16th		6 " Clothing do do	
	17th		5 " General Stores including 12 Wheels received and dumped at Railhead on account of "Thaw precautions."	

Geo Edwardes Lawrence
Captain D.A.D.O.S. 40th Division

WAR DIARY
or
INTELLIGENCE SUMMARY.

Army Form C. 2118.

Place	Date	Hour	Summary of Events and Information	Remarks and references to Appendices
	1917			
Bray sur Somme	Jan 18th	6 руб	Enemy aero reconn and dumped at Cachie	Heavy bombardment of Sm
	19th	10 "	do 4 Balloons. Heavy aero recon on the Somme sector	do
			were dumped at Cachie	do
	20th	4 "	Enemy aero recon and dumped at Cachie.	do
	21st	8 "	do do do	do
	22nd	5 "	do activity 84 machines seen shade fee	do
			Enemy aero recon and dumped at Cachie.	do
	23rd	4 "	Enemy aero recon and dumped at Cachie	do
	24th		No aero action	
	25th		do do Enemy for 6F5 engine and moved the	
			morning aero fifth into HAO Seen from Cachie.	
	26th	6 руб	Enemy aero recon and dumped at Cachie. Heavy bombardment of Sm	
	27th	5 "	do do do do do	do
	28th		No aero activity. Considerable sniping seen to north	

Re Edmonds Bureau

Captain
R.F.C. H.Q. Brigade

WAR DIARY or INTELLIGENCE SUMMARY.

Army Form C. 2118.

DADOS 40D Vol 10

Place	Date	Hour	Summary of Events and Information	Remarks and references to Appendices
Bray sur Somme	1917 March 1st		3 Tons of General Stores received and Issued.	
"	2nd		5 " " Clothing + Boots do do	
"	3rd		4 " " Horse Shoes do do	
"	4th 5th		No Stores received.	
"	6th		5 " " General Stores received and Issued.	
"	7th		6 " do do do	
"	8th		7 " do do do	
"	9th		6 " do do do	
"	10th		4 " do do do	
"	11th		6 " do do do	
"	12th		8 " do do do	
"	13th		3 " do do do	
"	14th		9 " do do do	
"	15th		4 " do do do	

Geo Edwardes-Lawrence
Captain
D.ADOS. 40th Division

WAR DIARY
or INTELLIGENCE SUMMARY.
(Erase heading not required.)

Army Form C. 2118.

Instructions regarding War Diaries and Intelligence Summaries are contained in F. S. Regs., Part II. and the Staff Manual respectively. Title pages will be prepared in manuscript.

Place	Date	Hour	Summary of Events and Information	Remarks and references to Appendices
	1917 March			
Bray sur Somme	16th		6 Tons of General Stores received & Issued.	
	17th		7 " " do do do	
	18th		5 " " do do do	
"	19th		10 " " do do do	
"	20th		11 " " do do do	
"	21st		12 " " do do do	
Curlu	22nd		5 " " do do do	
"	23rd		4 " " do do do	
"	24th		No Stores received.	
"	25th		264 Lews Boxes Magazines received & Issued	
"	26th		7 Tons of General Stores do do	
"	27th		4 " " do do do	
"	28th		3 " " do do do	
"	29th		24 Lewis Guns received and Issued.	

Geo Edwardes-Lawrence
Captain
D.A.D.O.S. 40th Division

T2134. Wt. W708—776. 500000. 4/15. Sir J. C. & S.

WAR DIARY
or
INTELLIGENCE SUMMARY.
(Erase heading not required.)

Army Form C. 2118.

Place	Date	Hour	Summary of Events and Information	Remarks and references to Appendices
Curlu	1917 March 30th		4 Tons of General Stores received and Issued.	
	31st		No Stores received.	

Geo Edwardes-Lawrence
Captain
D.A.D.O.S.
40th Division

WAR DIARY
or
INTELLIGENCE SUMMARY.

(Erase heading not required.)

Instructions regarding War Diaries and Intelligence Summaries are contained in F. S. Regs., Part II. and the Staff Manual respectively. Title pages will be prepared in manuscript.

Army Form C. 2118.

DADOS 40 D

Vol XI

Place	Date	Hour	Summary of Events and Information	Remarks and references to Appendices
Curlu.	1 4/17.		5 Tons of general stores Horseshoes Etc also 19 wheels received and issued. RAO.	
Curlu.	2 4/17.	.	No Trucks arrived. RAO.	
Curlu.	3 4/17.		5 Tons bulk clothing received and issued. RAO	
Curlu.	4 4/17.		4 Tons bulk Dubbing Etc. received and issued. RAO	
Curlu.	5 4/17.		No Trucks arrived. RAO.	
Curlu	6 4/17.		3 Tons bulk clothing Etc received and issued. RAO	
Curlu	7 4/17.		Left Curlu for Bouchevesnes - 5 Tons of Horseshoes Etc received and issued. RAO	

RAWilton. Condr. RAC.
a/c. a.d.o.s. 40th Div

2353 Wt. W2544/1454 700,000 5/15 D. D. & L. A.D.S.S. Forms/C. 2118.

WAR DIARY or INTELLIGENCE SUMMARY.

Army Form C. 2118.

(Erase heading not required.)

Place	Date	Hour	Summary of Events and Information	Remarks and references to Appendices
Bouchevesnes	8/4/16		6 Tons General Stores received and issued - RAO	
Bouchevesnes	9/4/16		No Trucks arrived. RAO	
Bouchevesnes	10/4/16		3½ Tons of Bulk Clothing received and issued - RAO	
Bouchevesnes	11/4/16		No Trucks arrived. RAO	
Bouchevesnes	12/4/16		12 Tons General Stores received and issued. Also two 18-Pr. Guns. - RAO	
Bouchevesnes	13/4/16		No Trucks arrived. RAO	
Bouchevesnes	14/4/16		6 Tons General Stores Horseshoes Etc received and issued RAO	
Bouchevesnes	15/4/16		No Trucks arrived. RAO	N.A. Hilton. Condr. R.A.S.C. a/k.a.D.O.P. 40th Div.

WAR DIARY
or
INTELLIGENCE SUMMARY

Army Form C. 2118.

Place	Date	Hour	Summary of Events and Information	Remarks and references to Appendices
Pondichum	16/4/19		Captain Geo. Edwards Ismain - Kinter arrested sick.	
			The stores arrived. R.O.	
Pondicherry	17/4/19		4 days bulk clothing received and issued. R.O.	
Pondicherry	18/4/19		The stores arrived. R.O.	
Pondicherry	19/4/19		Moved to Meerutaine - The trucks in - R.O.	
Meerutaine	20/4/19		4½ days bulk clothing received & issued. R.O.	
Meerutaine	21/4/19		The trucks arrived. R.O.	
Meerutaine	22/4/19		5 days frozen stores received & issued. R.O.	
Meerutaine	23/4/19		The trucks arrived. R.O.	
Meerutaine	24/4/19		5 days bulk clothing received and issued. R.O.	

… … **WAR DIARY** … … … Army Form C. 2118.
… … … or
Instructions regarding War Diaries and Intelligence … **INTELLIGENCE SUMMARY.**
Summaries are contained in F. S. Regs., Part II.
and the Staff Manual respectively. Title pages
will be prepared in manuscript. (Erase heading not required.)

Place	Date	Hour	Summary of Events and Information	Remarks and references to Appendices
Moislains	25/4/16		6 Tons General stores including 10 Wheels Etc and 2 Lewis Guns received and issued - R.A.O.	
Moislains	26/4/16		6 Lewis Guns received and issued - R.A.O.	
Moislains	27/4/16		2 Vickers Guns received and issued - R.A.O.	
Moislains	28/4/16		3½ Tons bulk clothing received and issued - R.A.O.	
Moislains	29/4/16		8 Tons Horseshoes, Box Respirators, + Wheels Etc received	
Moislains	30/4/16		1 Watertank received & issued no other stores —	

30th April 1917.

R.A.Kitton. Condr: R.O.C.
a/ D.A.D.O.S. 40th Divn.

WAR DIARY
or
INTELLIGENCE SUMMARY.

(Erase heading not required.)

Army Form C. 2118.

Place	Date	Hour	Summary of Events and Information	Remarks and references to Appendices
Pradelles	1/5/19		4 days general store received and issued -	Rain
"	2/5/19		No store received -	Rain
"	3/5/19		Moved Advance Depot to Rue. 4 days clothing received and issued. -	Rain
Rue	4/5/19		6 days bulk demands, pushing the received and issued -	Rain
Rue	5/5/19		No store received -	Rain
Rue	6/5/19		No store received -	Rain
Rue	7/5/19		8 days clothing received and issued. -	Rain
Rue	8/5/19		No store received -	Rain
Rue	9/5/19		No store received -	Rain

WAR DIARY or INTELLIGENCE SUMMARY.

Army Form C. 2118.

(Erase heading not required.)

Place	Date	Hour	Summary of Events and Information	Remarks and references to Appendices
Fins.	10/5/17		5 Tons of S.D. Clothing received and issued —	
Fins.	11th "		No stores received —	
Fins.	12th "		6 Tons of General Stores received and issued —	
Fins.	13th "		7 Tons Box Respirators and one 18 Pr: Gun received and issued —	
Fins	14th "		8 Tons Clothing received and issued —	
Fins	15th "		No stores received —	
Fins	16th "		1 – 18 Pr: ammn: wagon 1 – mess cart & 1 Water-cart received and issued no other stores —	
Fins	17th "		No stores received —	

Army Form C. 2118.

WAR DIARY
or
INTELLIGENCE SUMMARY.
(Erase heading not required.)

Instructions regarding War Diaries and Intelligence Summaries are contained in F.S. Regs., Part II. and the Staff Manual respectively. Title pages will be prepared in manuscript.

Place	Date	Hour	Summary of Events and Information	Remarks and references to Appendices
	June 18th		No steps received -	Ran
	June 19th		One day general stores received and issued -	Ran
	June 20th		No stores received -	Ran
	June 21st		6 days of clothing received and issued -	Rain
	June 22nd		No stores received -	Rain
	June 23rd		14 cases N.A. Medical received. No complete issue -	Rain
	June 24th		3 days of clothing received & issued -	Rain
	June 25th		No stores received -	Rain

2333 Wt.W25441151 700,000 5/15 D.D.&L. A.D.S.S.Forms/C 2118.

WAR DIARY or INTELLIGENCE SUMMARY.

Army Form C. 2118.

(Erase heading not required.)

Place	Date	Hour	Summary of Events and Information	Remarks and references to Appendices
Yins	26th		7 Tons Horseshoes & Dubbing Etc received and issued —	RSO
Yins	27th		No Stores received. —	RSO
Yins	28th		5 Tons of general stores including 300 Tubs washing received & issued. —	RSO
Yins	29th		7 Tons general stores received & issued —	RSO
Yins	30th		2½ Tons Oil & grease received & issued. —	RSO
Yins	31st		8 Tons General stores received & issued —	RSO

R.A. Kitson. Con 40 110
A/L.a.s.o. 40th Div

WAR DIARY
or
INTELLIGENCE SUMMARY.
(Erase heading not required.)

Army Form C. 2118.

Instructions regarding War Diaries and Intelligence Summaries are contained in F. S. Regs., Part II. and the Staff Manual respectively. Title pages will be prepared in manuscript.

DADOS 40 D

Vol 13

Place	Date	Hour	Summary of Events and Information	Remarks and references to Appendices
	1917			
Fins	June 16th		3½ Tons of Clothing received and issued.	
"	" 17th		No Stores received.	
"	" 18th		do do	
"	" 19th		2½ Tons of Clothing received and issued.	
"	" 20th		No Stores received.	
"	" 21st		do do	
"	" 22nd		6 Tons of Horse shoes, Dubbing etc received and issued.	
"	" 23rd		3 " of Clothing received and issued.	
"	" 24th		5 " " General Stores received and issued. Also 300 Suits washing 3½ falls.	
"	" 25th		No Stores received.	
"	" 26th		6 Tons of General Stores received and issued.	
"	" 27th		2 " " Clothing do do	
"	" 28th		1.350 Helmets P.H. received.	
"	" 29th		9 Tons of Horse shoes, 1 Cart Water & 1 Gun & Limber received and issued.	
"	" 30th		3 " " Clothing received and issued.	
"			Geo Edwardes-Lawrence	
			Captain D.A.D.O.S.	
			40th Division	

T2134. Wt. W708—776. 500000. 4/15. Sir J. C. & S.

WAR DIARY or INTELLIGENCE SUMMARY.

Army Form C. 2118.

Place	Date	Hour	Summary of Events and Information	Remarks and references to Appendices
	1917			
Tino	June 1st		6 Tons of Clothing received and issued also 93 Tins Water carriage.	
"	" 2nd		7 " " Horse Shoes do do.	
"	" 3rd		No Stores received.	
"	" 4th		3 Tons of General Stores received and issued.	
"	" 5th		4 " " do do do	
"	" 6th		No Stores received.	
"	" 7th		do do	
"	" 8th		8 Tons of Horse Shoes received and issued.	
"	" 9th		6 " " General Stores do do also 3 T M Guns.	
"	" 10th		7 " " do do do.	
"	" 11th		5 " " Picketing gear and stable necessaries.	
"	" 12th		No Stores received.	
"	" 13th		4 Tons of Clothing received and issued.	
"	" 14th		6 " " General Stores received and issued.	
"	" 15th		63 Boxes of Horse Shoes & 1 bag of Horse nails received and issued.	

Geo Edwardes-Lawrence
Captain   D.A.D.O.S.
40th Division

WAR DIARY or INTELLIGENCE SUMMARY

Army Form C. 2118.

Paris H.Q. G4/14

Place	Date	Hour	Summary of Events and Information	Remarks and references to Appendices
two	1917 July 1st		1 double Cart and 1 G.S. Wagon received and issued.	
	2nd		5 tons of Ferrous Stores, 6 bales of Blankets and 2 Canopies 18 G's received & issued	
	3"	4½ "	Clothing received and issued	
	4"	6 "	Ferrous Stores received and issued	
	5"	5 "	Horseshoes & Box Cylinders received and issued.	
	6"	3 "	Clothing received and issued.	
	7"		No Stores received	
	8"	4 "	Ferrous Stores received and issued	
	9"	2½ "	Clothing do do	
	10"		No Stores received	
	11"	4 "	Ferrous Stores received and issued	
	12"	2½ "	Clothing do do	
	13"	4 "	Horseshoes do do	
	14"	4 "	Ferrous Stores do do	
	15"	4 "	do do do do	

Eta Ebanks-Tamerine
Caspian Bases. A.A. Moore

WAR DIARY or **INTELLIGENCE SUMMARY.**
(Erase heading not required.)

Army Form C. 2118.

Place	Date	Hour	Summary of Events and Information	Remarks and references to Appendices
Tins	1917 July 16th		2 Tons of Clothing received and issued.	
"	17th		No Stores received.	
"	18th		15 Tons of General Stores received and issued.	
"	19th		No Stores received.	
"	20th		2½ Tons of Clothing received and issued.	
"	21st		No stores received.	
"	22nd		3 Tons of General Stores received and issued.	
"	23rd		5 " " Clothing etc do do. also 2 Guns How: 4.5 with carriages and limbers complete.	
"	24th		1 Carriage Fd. 18 Pr received and issued.	
"	25th		4 Tons of General Stores received and issued.	
"	26th		4 " " Horseshoes do do. also 2 Vickers Guns.	
"	27th		5 Tons of Clothing and 8 Tables received and issued also 1 How: Carriage.	

Geo Edwardes-Lawrence
Captain. D.A.D.O.S. 40th Division.

WAR DIARY
or
INTELLIGENCE SUMMARY.

(Erase heading not required.)

Army Form C. 2118.

Instructions regarding War Diaries and Intelligence Summaries are contained in F. S. Regs., Part II. and the Staff Manual respectively. Title pages will be prepared in manuscript.

Place	Date	Hour	Summary of Events and Information	Remarks and references to Appendices
Fino	1917 July 28th		5 Tons of General Stores, 1 Hand Cart & 1 Limber Wagon received and issued.	
"	29th		4 " " " " " received and issued.	
"	30th		3 Lewis Guns received and issued.	
"	31st		1½ Tons of Clothing received and issued.	
			Geo Edwards-Lawrence	
			Captain	
			D.A.D.O.S.	
			40th Division.	

T2134. Wt. W708—776. 500000. 4/15. Sir J. C. & S.

WAR DIARY or INTELLIGENCE SUMMARY

(Erase heading not required.)

Army Form C. 2118.

DADOS 40D

Vol 15

Place	Date 1917	Hour	Summary of Events and Information	Remarks and references to Appendices
	August			
Tons	1st		5 Tons of Stores received and issued.	
"	2nd & 3rd		No Stores received	
"	4th		7 Tons of Horse shoes and General Stores received and issued.	
"	5th		6 " " Clothing do do	
"	6th & 7th		No Stores received	
"	8th		3 Tons of Clothing received and issued.	
"	9th		8 " " Horse shoes, Wheels etc received and issued	
"	10th		No stores received.	
"	11th		3 Tons of General Stores, & 21 Bicycles received and issued.	
"	12th		8 " " do do received and issued.	
"	13th		3 " " Clothing do do	
"	14th		5 " " Horseshoes received and issued.	
"	15th		5 " " General Stores, 12 Wheels etc. received and issued	
"	16th		3 " " Clothing received and issued.	
"	17th		No Stores received.	

Geo Edwardes-Lawrence
Captain DADOS
40th Division.

WAR DIARY
or
INTELLIGENCE SUMMARY

Army Form C. 2118.

Place	Date 1917	Hour	Summary of Events and Information	Remarks and references to Appendices
Cropard	August 18th		6 sets of general stores received and issued	
"	19th		3 " do do do do	
"	20th		6 " Clothing do do	
"	21st		6 " Stores do do	
"	22nd		No stores received	
"	23rd		5 sets of clothing received and issued	
"	24th		324 Jump Drum do do	
"	25th		8 sets of general stores received and issued	
"	26th		No stores received	
"	27th		2 sets of clothing received and issued	
"	28th		612 Jump Drum do do	
"	29th		4 sets of Stores do do	
"	30th		2 " Haversacks do do	
"	31st		2 " Clothing do do	

Eric Edwards-Lawson
Captain
25.9.05
40th Division.

WAR DIARY or INTELLIGENCE SUMMARY

DADOS 40D
Vol 16

Place	Date	Hour	Summary of Events and Information	Remarks and references to Appendices
	1917 Sept.			
Tins	1st		6 Tons of Stores received and issued.	
"	2nd		3 " " do do do also 1 Mess Cart.	
"	3rd		6 " " do do do.	
"	4th		8 " " do do do also 24 Wheels.	
"	5th		4 " " do do do.	
"	6th		2½ " " do do do.	
"	7th		No Stores received.	
"	8th		2 Tons of Stores received and issued, also 1 Watercart.	
"	9th		5 " " do do do.	
"	10th		3 " " do do do.	
"	11th		No Stores received.	
"	12th		5 Tons of Stores received and issued.	
"	13th		3½ " " do do do.	
"	14th		No Stores received.	
"	15th		10 Tons of Stores received and issued.	

Geo Edwardes-Lawrence
Captain DADOS
40th Division

WAR DIARY
or
INTELLIGENCE SUMMARY.

(Erase heading not required.)

Army Form C. 2118.

Instructions regarding War Diaries and Intelligence Summaries are contained in F. S. Regs., Part II. and the Staff Manual respectively. Title pages will be prepared in manuscript.

Place	Date	Hour	Summary of Events and Information	Remarks and references to Appendices
Iino	1917			
	8th May		No Sano recruits	
	16th			
	17th	4120	Party. Horse recruits and scout	
	18th		No Sano recruits	
	19th	4.30	8 Sano recruits and scout	
	20th	6 "	do do do do	
	21st	6 "	do do do do	
	22nd	5 "	do do do do	
	23rd		No Sano recruits	
	24th	3 and	3 Sano recruits and scout	
		abo 3b "	Winds interrupting recruit.	
	25th	4 "	Sano recruits and scout	
	26th		No Sano recruits	
	27	10 am	Sano recruits and scout	
		abo 1600	8 hrs for carrying Kaka ascent	

Leo Edwards-Fanen
Captain
J.J.O.T.
110" Division.

WAR DIARY or INTELLIGENCE SUMMARY

Army Form C. 2118.

Place	Date	Hour	Summary of Events and Information	Remarks and references to Appendices
Fins	1917 Sept 28th		No Stores received.	
"	29th		6 Tons of Stores received and issued, also rear portion of a Field Kitchen	
"	30th		16,000 Blankets received and issued	
"	"		also 23 Tons of Winter underclothing received.	

Geo Edwardes-Lawrence
Captain
D.A.D.O.S.
40th Division

WAR DIARY
or
INTELLIGENCE SUMMARY

Army Form C. 2118.

Place	Date	Hour	Summary of Events and Information	Remarks and references to Appendices
Arras	1917 October 1st	1ᵖᵐ	3 tons of stone metal and sand	
"	"	8ᵃᵐ	No stone metal	
"	"	3³⁰	4 tons of stone metal and sand	
"	"	4ᵖᵐ	6 " do do do.	
"	"	5ᵖᵐ	No stone metal	
"	"	7ᵖᵐ	6 tons of stone metal and sand	
"	"	8+⁷	some pieces sent from the Base. do	
"	"	7+⁸	do do do do.	Demanding
"	"	11ᵖᵐ	8 tons of stone metal and sand	for Base
"	"	12ᵖᵐ	7 " do do do	
"	"	12³⁰	7 " do do do.	
"	"	13³⁰	5 " do do do.	
"	"	14ᵖᵐ	14 " do do do.	
"	"	15ᵖᵐ	No stone metal	
"	"	16ᵖᵐ	No stone metal	
"	"	17ᵖᵐ	4 tons of stone metal and sand	

For Charlie Lemoine Calkarn

WAR DIARY or INTELLIGENCE SUMMARY

Army Form C. 2118.

DADOS 40 D

Vol 17

Place	Date	Hour	Summary of Events and Information	Remarks and references to Appendices
Beaumetz les Loges	1917 October 18th		No Stores received.	
"	19th		12 Tons of Stores received and issued.	
"	20th		12,500 Blankets do do.	
"	21st		8 Tons of Stores do do	
"	22nd		No Stores received.	
"	23rd		20 Tons of Stores received and issued.	
"	24th		No Stores received.	
"	25th & 26th		Issues suspended from the Base.	
"	27th & 28th		do do do do.	
"	29th		6 Tons of Stores received and issued.	
"	30th		7 " " do do do.	
Moncheaux	31st		No Stores received.	

Geo Edwardes-Lawrence
Captain
D.A.D.O.S.
40th Division.

WAR DIARY
INTELLIGENCE SUMMARY

Lt: Colonel Farquhar
Calhoun 2835 40th Infantry

Place	Date 1917	Hour	Summary of Events and Information	Remarks and references to Appendices
Monchy	1st+2nd		No shells heard	
"	3rd		24 T.M. Howitzers heard and seen	
"	4th		No shells heard	
"	5th			
Cambrai	6th		6 rounds of shells heard and seen	
"	7th		No shells heard	
"	8th		do do	
"	9th+10th		6 rounds of shells heard and seen	
"	11th		No shells heard	
"	12th		6 rounds of shells heard and seen	
"	13th		9 " do do	
La Harlière	14th		12 " do do	
"	15th		6 " do do	
"	16th		No shells heard	
"	17th		5 rounds of shells heard and seen	
Broadwaud	18th		10 " do do	
"	19th		9 " do do	
"	20th		do do	
"	21st		No shells heard	
"	22nd		4 rounds of shells heard and seen	

Place	Date 1917	Hour	Summary of Events and Information	Remarks and references to Appendices
Beaulencourt	Nov. 23rd		8 Tons of Stores received and issued.	
"	24th		3 " do do do.	
"	25th		No Stores received.	
"	26th		4 Tons of Stores received and issued.	
Beaumetz les Loges	27th		No Stores received.	
"	28th		do do	
"	29th		200 Lamps. F.S. received.	
"	30th		No Stores received.	

Geo Edwardes-Lawrence
Captain
D.A.D.O.S.
40th Division

WAR DIARY
or
INTELLIGENCE SUMMARY

Army Form C. 2118.

Place	Date 1917	Hour	Summary of Events and Information	Remarks and references to Appendices
Beaumaris to Patio Sardina	Dec 1st		Watched out 1 junkers F.S. large fa 19" Kapp Hotel Apolda W.1 & towed	
	2nd		5 tons of gas mined and sown	
	3rd		" " " Beaumaris to Patio & Sardinia. No gas mined	
	4th		8 tons of gas mined and sown	
	5th		" 8 " do do	
	6th		No gas mined	
	7th		8 tons of gas mined and sown	
	8th		" 19 " do do	
	9th		" 9 " do do	
	10th		Watched in F Batt 177 Bde R.A. and 1st N. 17th Welch Regt mined and sown	
	11th		7 tons of gas mined and sown	
	12th		Watched in Fa 20." Middlesex Regt & watched fa C/177 Bde R.A. mined and sown	
	12½		4½ tons of gas mined and sown	
	13th		" 7 " do do	
	14th		" 5 " do do 028 29 Feb (?)	
	15th		" 10 " do do	
	16th		" 8 " do do	
	17th		" 10 " do do	
	18th		No gas mined	
	19th		17 tons of gas mined and sown	

WAR DIARY or INTELLIGENCE SUMMARY.

Army Form C. 2118.

(*Erase heading not required.*)

Place	Date 1917	Hour	Summary of Events and Information	Remarks and references to Appendices
Erviller	Dec 20th		8 Tons of Stores received and issued.	
"	21st		No Stores received.	
"	22nd		8 Tons of Stores received and issued.	
"	23rd		6 " do do do.	
"	24th		5 " do do do.	
"	25th		8 " do do do.	
"	26th		No Stores received.	
"	27th		7 Tons of Stores received and issued.	
"	28th		12 " do do do.	
"	29th		20 " do do do.	
"	30th		8 " do do do.	
"	31st		5 " do do do.	

Geo. Edwardes Lawrence
Captain
D.A.D.O.S.
40th Division

Original   2 sheets   1st sheet

WAR DIARY
or
INTELLIGENCE SUMMARY.

Army Form C. 2118.

Instructions regarding War Diaries and Intelligence
Summaries are contained in F. S. Regs., Part II.
and the Staff Manual respectively. Title pages
will be prepared in manuscript.

(Erase heading not required.)

DADOS 40D

Place	Date 1918	Hour	Summary of Events and Information	Remarks and references to Appendices
Ervillers	Jan. 1st		5 Tons of Stores received and issued.	
"	2nd		7 " do do do	
"	3rd		8 " do do do	
"	4th		No Stores received.	
"	5th		6 Tons of Stores received and issued.	
"	6th		No Stores received	
"	7th		8 Tons of Stores received and issued. also two 18 Pdrs	
"	8th		12 " do do do do one 18 Pdr	
"	9th		4 " do do do do one Lewis Gun	
"	10th		6 " do do do do one 18 Pdr	
"	11th		4 " do do do do Two Pr Carriages	
"	12th		No Stores received.	
"	13th		One Lewis Gun received and issued.	
"	14th		9 Tons of Stores received and issued, also one Lewis Gun	
"	15th		3½ " do do do.	
"	16th		4 " do do do.	
"	17th		No Stores received.	

Geo Edwardes-Lawrence
Captain
D. a. D. O. S.
40th Division.

A5834   Wt. W4973/M687   750,000   8/16   D. D. & L. Ltd.   Forms/C.2118/13.

WAR DIARY or **INTELLIGENCE SUMMARY.**

Army Form C. 2118.

Original — 2 Sheets — 2nd Sheet.

Instructions regarding War Diaries and Intelligence Summaries are contained in F. S. Regs., Part II. and the Staff Manual respectively. Title pages will be prepared in manuscript.

(*Erase heading not required.*)

Place	Date	Hour	Summary of Events and Information	Remarks and references to Appendices
	18/1/18		No Stores Received	
Ervillers	19/1/18		5 Tons clothing received and issued —	R.H.
"	20/1/18		12 Tons Horseshoes Etc received & Issued —	R.H.
"	21/1/18		6 Tons Respirators and general stores received and issued —	R.H.
"	22/1/18		8 Tons clothing received and Issued —	R.H.
"	23/1/18		No stores received —	R.H.
"	24/1/18		7 Tons Wheels Etc received and Issued —	R.H.
"	25/1/18		9 Tons clothing received and Issued —	R.H.
"	26/1/18		No stores received —	R.H.
"	27/1/18		No stores received —	R.H.
"	28/1/18		3 Tons clothing received & issued —	R.H.
"	29/1/18		5 Tons general stores received & issued —	R.H.
"	30/1/18		No stores received —	R.H.
"	31/1/18		No stores received —	R.H.

31/1/18.

R.D. Hilton.
Condr. A.O.C.
a/D.A.D.O.S. Lobien:

WAR DIARY
or
INTELLIGENCE SUMMARY

(Erase heading not required.)

Army Form C. 2118.

RA & FSHQ (?)

Place	Date 1918	Hour	Summary of Events and Information	Remarks and references to Appendices
Evuillers	Nov 1st		No firing occurred	
	2nd			
	3rd	10 am	8 shrap: incendiary, 14 HE shell, 2 armed and some	
	4 "		do do unarmed and some	
	5 "		No firing occurred	
	6 "		3 rnds f. shrap unarmed and some	
	7 "	8 "	do do do do	
	8 "		No firing occurred	
	9 "		3 rnds f. shrap unarmed and some	
			Gunbar Reg? Finished fuzes F.S. Hand held fuzes F.S. and in takes	
	10 "		Cold unarmed and some	
	11 "		No firing occurred	
	12 "		10 rnds f. shrap unarmed and some	
		3½ "	do do do do	
	13 "		No firing occurred	
	14 "		3 rnds f. shrap unarmed and some	
	15 "		9 " do do do	
	16 "			
	17 "		No firing occurred	
	18 "		do	
	"		6 rnds 8 shrap: incendiary, 14 HE shell, 225 Yellow Ease Unarmed and some	
			26 Browning unarmed and some	
			Reference Division	
			Column 32850 No 'C' Series	

Buiny Artillery

WAR DIARY or INTELLIGENCE SUMMARY

DADOS 40D Vol 22

Army Form C. 2118.

Place	Date 1918	Hour	Summary of Events and Information	Remarks and references to Appendices
Beaumetz les Loges	March 1st		No Stores received.	
"	2nd		8 Tons of Stores received and issued	
"	3rd		No Stores received. D.A.D.O.S. left for a course of instruction on Ammunition	
"	4th		5 Tons of Stores received and issued.	
"	5th		No Stores received.	
"	6th		5 Tons of Stores received and issued.	
"	7th		} No Stores received	
"	8th			
"	9th		3 Tons of Stores received and issued.	
"	10th		No Stores received	
"	11th		4 Tons of Stores received and issued.	
"	12th		7 " do do do	
"	13th		Moved to Boiry St Rictrude	

Ho Edwards Lawrence
Captain D.A.D.O.S. "40" Division

WAR DIARY
or
INTELLIGENCE SUMMARY

Army Form C. 2118.

Place	Date 1918	Hour	Summary of Events and Information	Remarks and references to Appendices
Berin SReduto	14th Mar		8 gave of flares missed and Green	
"	15"		3 " do do do	
"	16"		No flares seen	
"	17"		do do	
"	18"		Westward + 1 Bunker rocket greens and green	
"	19"		2 gave of flares greens and green	
"	20"		do do do	
"	21"		do do do	
"	22nd			
Afunda	23rd		Moves to Afunda. No flares general	
"	24"		Moved to Bunguin. Fires orgina on confirmed ammunition camps.	
Bunguin	25"		Moved to Famake + Stand Effect at 2.30 am moved to Hanimesent	
Hanim- esent Camp	"		Arrived at Hanimesent.	
	26"		General and count to detain June K 40. Machine gun fire severely 2.5" Ordered to move to Ostamieta. Then recommitted of 2.30 AM 26" ordered to move to Gumner.	

Jo Edwards-Jourdan
Captain

WAR DIARY or INTELLIGENCE SUMMARY.

(Erase heading not required.)

Army Form C. 2118.

Place	Date 1918	Hour	Summary of Events and Information	Remarks and references to Appendices
Pommier	March 26th		Wire received at 6.30 PM to move to Saulty. Movement completed at 2.30 AM on the 27th inst. No Stores received.	
Saulty	27th		Issued 5 Lewis Guns to 10/11th H.L. Infy.	
"	28th		do 4 Vickers " " 40th M.G. Bn.	
"	29th		Transferred to XIII Corps.	
"	30th		Received and Issued at 2.45 AM 6 running out springs for 18 Bs 1 Trigger & extractor 18 Bs to keep guns in action.	
"	31st		Moved to Merville. Transferred to XV Corps. Received and issued 42 Lewis Guns to 120th Brigade. do do 17 Vickers " " 40th M.G. Bn.	

Geo Edwardes Johnson
Captain
D.A.D.O.S.
40th Division

WAR DIARY or INTELLIGENCE SUMMARY

Army Form C. 2118.

Place	Date 1918	Hour	Summary of Events and Information	Remarks and references to Appendices
Marsille	April 1st		100 Extra Gunners and 17 drivers arrived and came marched to C.R.A. 5th Army.	
C.R.A. 5th Army	2nd		3½ guns and ammunition column	
	3rd		do do do also 23 Gunners & 6 Sub + Q.M.S.	
	4th		Second bombardment. No fit Walking wounded arrived and came.	
	5th		8 guns & ammunition and column	
	6th		11 do do do	
	7th		7 do do do	
	8th		12 do do	
			de reinforcements with the Officers Nr 2 and Nr sent reinst to Lieut Baudoin.	
Lieut Baudoin	9th		Have of 10 Gunner marching to Ebergsele	
	10th		marched to Esemy	
Arnieres Hazebrouck	11th		marched to Hazebrouck. Star A Battery marching	
	12th		16 extra Gunners arrived and came	
	13th		30 do do do Star A Battery marching	
Ebergsele	14th		marched to Ebergsele a Coy Gunners J Offs + drivers came and come marched to Serbia in Ford	
			do Lieut Baudoin	

Paris 5404

JH 93

WAR DIARY or INTELLIGENCE SUMMARY

Army Form C. 2118.

(Erase heading not required.)

Place	Date 1918	Hour	Summary of Events and Information	Remarks and references to Appendices
St Martin au faert	April 15th		15 Trucks of Stores received and issued as far as possible	
"	16th		1 Officers mess Cart for 21st Middlesex Regt + 1 Cart Maltese for Div. Signals received and issued	
"	17th		2 Hand portions Limbers, 2 Wagons G.S. 6 Watercarts + 1 Maltese Carts received and issued.	
"	18th		5 Tons of Stores received and issued, also 109 Lewis Guns.	
"	19th		10 Bicycles, 40 Cases of Box Respirators, 2 Ambulance Wagons, 20 Lewis + 21 Vickers Guns	
"	20th		300 Rifles, 8 Tons of Stores, 3 Watercarts, 1 Maltese Cart, 1 Kitchen travelling body and received and issued	
"	"		1 Vickers Gun received and issued.	
"	21st		Moved to Wozennes.	
Wozennes	22nd		8 Limbers G.S. Wagons, 3 Watercarts, 2 Trucks of Pontoon parts, 2500 Blankets, 1 Maltese Cart, 4 Field Kitchens received and issued.	
"	23rd		21 Tons of Stores & 3 Limbered Wagons received and issued.	
"	24th		3 Limbered Wagons, 1 Pontoon Wagon, 2 Field Kitchens + 2 Field Kitchen bodies received and issued.	
"	25th		8 Tons of Stores received and issued.	
"	26th		6 Field Kitchens do do	
"	27th		10 Tons of Stores do do	
"	28th		3 " " do do do	
"	29th		5 " " do do do	
"	30th		No Stores received	

Jos Edwardes Jansens
Major D.A.D.O.S.
40th Division

WAR DIARY
or
INTELLIGENCE SUMMARY

Army Form C. 2118.

Place	Date	Hour	Summary of Events and Information	Remarks and references to Appendices
Warloy	May 1918			
	1st		13 June Officers and 1 Killen Drivers, 184 Other ranks and 505 horses en Spare mules	
	2nd			
	3rd		29 Bicycles, carts and ammunition to the Base.	
	4"		3 June Officers, 12 Other ranks and 333 horses en spare mules	
	5+6"			
	7+8"		No Spare mules } Some supplies for the Base do	
	9"		} Units obtaining hard equipment do	
	10"		2 June Officers, 12 Other ranks and 336 horses	
	11"		3 do Garrison trade Officers and horses	
			1 Cart. With four Other ranks and horses	
Etrechy	12"		6 June Officers, 17 Other ranks and horses	
	13"		Horses to Etrechy	
Ebbingham	14"		8 June Officers, Officers and horses	
	15"		No Spare mules	
	16"		do do do	
	17"		do do do	

Eto Edwards – Lawson.

Major General
Comdg 40th Division.

Paras Army 24

WAR DIARY or INTELLIGENCE SUMMARY

Army Form C. 2118.

Place	Date 1918	Hour	Summary of Events and Information	Remarks and references to Appendices
Ebblinghem	May 18th		3 Tons of Stores received and issued.	
"	19th		No Stores received.	
"	20th		do do	
"	21st		1 Cart Water Tank received and issued.	
"	22nd		4 Tons of Stores received and issued.	
"	23rd		No Stores received.	
"	24th		do do	
"	25th		5 Tons of Stores received and issued.	
"	26th		4 Carts Tool R.E. for 432nd Coy R.E. reconsigned to Stanton Railhead.	
"	"		4 Tons of Stores received and issued.	
"	27th		No Stores received.	
"	28th		Carts Officers Mess 1 received and issued.	
"	29th		4 Tons of Stores received and issued.	
"	30th		No Stores received.	
"	31st		do do	

Geo Edwardes-Lawrence
Major
D.A.D.O.S. 40th Division

WAR DIARY
or
INTELLIGENCE SUMMARY

Army Form C. 2118.

PAPAS 14 DIV Feb 25

Place	Date 1918	Hour	Summary of Events and Information	Remarks and references to Appendices
Mulhuysen	Feb 1		3 tons of stores issued and 2 some do	
	2nd		3 do do do do	
	3rd		no stores issued	
	4		5 tons of stores issued and issued	
	5		3 " do do do	
	6		no stores issued	
	7		do do	
	8		3 tons of stores issued and issued	
	9		no movements	
	10		1 Cart Cable issued and issued	
	11		3 tons of stores issued and issued	
	12		2.12 tons of Equipment issued and issued	
	13		1½ tons of 4 tons ammunition issued	
	14		24 Feb do do do	
	15		no stores issued	
	16/17		3 tons of stores issued and issued	
	18		no movements	
			4 tons of Ammunition and issued	

Edmondo-Lanoux
Major 2nd 2 yr 48th Division

WAR DIARY or INTELLIGENCE SUMMARY.

Army Form C. 2118.

Place	Date 1918	Hour	Summary of Events and Information	Remarks and references to Appendices
Ebblinghem	June 19th		3 Tons of Stores received and issued.	
"	20th		72 Lewis Guns do do.	
"	21st		24 3" Stokes do do to 3 Trench Mortar Batteries.	
"	"		3 Tons of Stores received and issued.	
"	22nd		9 " " do do do.	
"	23rd		5 " " do do do.	
"	24th		No Stores received.	
"	25th		2 Tons of Stores received and issued.	
"	26th		6 " " do do do.	
"	27th		5 " " do do do.	
"	28th		No Stores received.	
"	29th		5 Tons of Stores received and issued.	
"	30th		6 " " do do do	

Geo Edwardes-Lawrence
Major
D.A.D.O.S.
40th Division

WAR DIARY
or
INTELLIGENCE SUMMARY

Army Form C. 2118.

40th Division.

Place	Date 1918	Hour	Summary of Events and Information	Remarks and references to Appendices
Ebblinghem	July 1st		3 guns 9 shells nizard and round	
"	2nd		no shells nizard	
"	3rd		4 guns 9 shells nizard and round	
"	4th		3 do do do do also 31 whizbangs	
"	5th		no shells nizard	
"	6th		8 guns 9 shells nizard and round	
"	7th		no shells nizard	
"	8th		10 guns 9 shells nizard and round also 37 Strayers	
"	9th		no shells nizard	
"	10th		28 whizbangs nizard and round also 1 large persters 4.8	
"	11th		11 guns 9 shells nizard and round	
"	12th		no shells nizard	
"	13th		3 guns 9 shells nizard and round by the Germans	
"	14th		6 guns 9 shells nizard and round	
"	15th		4 " do do do	
"	16th		no shells nizard	
"	17th		4 guns 9 shells nizard and round	

WAR DIARY or INTELLIGENCE SUMMARY

Army Form C. 2118.

Place	Date July	Hour	Summary of Events and Information	Remarks and references to Appendices
Ebblinghem	18th		No Stores received.	
"	19th		30 Bicycles received and issued.	
"	20th		3 Tons of Stores received and issued.	
"	21st		21 Bicycles do do.	
"	22nd		No Stores received.	
"	23rd		4 Tons of Stores received and issued.	
"	24th		No Stores received.	
"	25th		3 Tons of Stores received and issued.	
"	26th		4 " do do do.	
"	27th		No Stores received.	
"	28th		27 Complete Field Kitchens received and issued, & 27 G.S. Limbered Wagons sent to the Base.	
"	29th		4 do do do do.	
"	30th		No Stores received.	
"	31st		do do.	

Geo Edwardes-Lawrence
Major
D.A.D.O.S.
40th Division

WAR DIARY
or
INTELLIGENCE SUMMARY

Army Form C. 2118.

(Erase heading not required.)

Ho: 9 Divisn.
2.8.25

Place	Date 1918	Hour	Summary of Events and Information	Remarks and references to Appendices
Billinghem	August 1st		8 trns of steno recvd and sent	
		2nd	No steno recvd	
		3rd	5 trns of steno recvd and sent	
		"	No steno recvd	
		5th	3 trns of steno recvd and sent	
		6+7	No steno recvd	
		8"	6 trns of steno recvd and sent	
		9"	No steno recvd	
		10"	6 trns of steno recvd and sent	
		11"	7 " " " " do	
		12"	1 light case cart recvd and sent to 40" Div Sigmls RE	
		13+14	No steno recvd	
		15"	8 trns of steno recvd and sent	
		16"	No steno recvd	

Rio Edwardio-Janeiro
July

WAR DIARY or INTELLIGENCE SUMMARY

Army Form C. 2118.

Place	Date 1918	Hour	Summary of Events and Information	Remarks and references to Appendices
Ebblinghem	August 17th		8 Tons of Stores received and issued.	
"	18th		No Stores received.	
"	19th		9 Tons of Stores received and issued.	
"	20th & 21st		No Stores received.	
"	22nd		8 Tons of Stores received and issued.	
"	23rd		No Stores received.	
"	24th		4 Tons of Stores received and issued. Moved to Wallon Cappel.	
Wallon Cappel	25th		No Stores received.	
"	26th		5 Tons of Stores received and issued.	
"	27th & 28th		No Stores received.	
"	29th		4 Tons of Stores received and issued.	
"	30th		5 " do do do.	
Hazebrouck	31st		2 " do do do.	

Geo Edwardes-Jameson
Major
D.A.D.O.S.
40th Division.

WAR DIARY
or
INTELLIGENCE SUMMARY

Army Form C. 2118.

PARIS 4 J/8/28

Place	Date	Hour	Summary of Events and Information	Remarks and references to Appendices
Hazebrouck	Sept 1 1918	8:30 pm	3 lots of flares ignited and burnt.	
"	2nd		No flares ignited.	
"	3rd		do. do. Word has been sent to Lt Wyatt.	
Lt Wyatt	4th		6 lots of flares ignited and burnt.	
"	5 "		No flares ignited.	
"	6 "		3 lots of flares ignited and burnt also 1 extinct.	
"	7 "		No flares ignited.	
"	8 "		4 lots of flares ignited and burnt	
"	9 "		4 " do do do	
"	10 & 11 "		No flares ignited	
"	12 "		3 lots of flares ignited and burnt	
"	13 "		3 lots of flares ignited and burnt	
"	14 "		5 lots of flares ignited and burnt	
"	15 "		No flares ignited.	

Lt Edwards-Gavin
Maje
J R B S
H.Q. Ypres.

WAR DIARY or INTELLIGENCE SUMMARY

Army Form C. 2118.

(Erase heading not required.)

Place	Date 1918	Hour	Summary of Events and Information	Remarks and references to Appendices
near La Motte	Sept 16th		One G.S. Wagon, 1 Limber Wagon + 13 Lewis Guns received and issued. Moved to Steenwerck	
Steenwerck	17th		4 Tons of Stores received and issued.	
"	18th		No Stores received.	
"	19th		5 Tons of Stores received and issued, also 5 Lewis Guns.	
"	20th		1 Lewis Gun received and issued.	
"	21st		10 Tons of Stores received and issued.	
"	22nd		No Stores received.	
"	23rd		8 Tons of Stores received and issued.	
"	24 & 25		No Stores received.	
"	26th		5 Tons of Stores received and issued.	
"	27th		8 " do do do.	
"	28th		No Stores received.	
"	29th		1 Lewis Gun received and issued.	
"	30th		4 Tons of Stores received and issued.	

Geo Edwardes-Lawrence
Major
D.A.D.O.S. 40th Division.

WAR DIARY
or
INTELLIGENCE SUMMARY

Army Form C. 2118.

Place	Date 1918	Hour	Summary of Events and Information	Remarks and references to Appendices
Alnwick	1st		70 3lero winced	
	2nd		6 3ero 3 lero winced and issued	
	3rd		70 3lero winced	
	4th		119 Boots 3 Jacks & Drawers winced and issued	
	5th		6 3ero 3 lero winced and issued	
	6th		4 " " do " also 1 3ero 3ero	
	7th		120 Boots 3 Jacks & Drawers winced and issued also 4 3ero 3ero	
	8th		9 3ero 3ero winced and issued	
	9th		70 3lero winced	
	10th		6 3ero 3 lero winced and issued	
	11th		4 " " do " do "	
	12th		5 3ero 3 lero do also 130 Blankets to complete 15 3ero 3ero pr man	
	13th		4 " do do " also 1 3ero 3ero	
	14th		70 3lero winced	
	15th		3 3ero 3ero winced and issued	

Lee Enfield - Known

Major J.J.J.J.
HQ Division

WAR DIARY

Army Form C. 2118.

Place	Date 1918	Hour	Summary of Events and Information	Remarks and references to Appendices
	October			
Steenwerck	16th		12 Tons of Stores received and issued.	
"	17th		1 Lewis Gun do do	
"	18th		4 Tons of Stores do do also 1 Vickers Gun.	
"	19th		No Stores received – Moved to Armentieres.	
Armentieres	20th		15 Tons of Stores received and issued.	
"	21st		No Stores received.	
Wambrechies	22nd		3 Trucks of Jerkins & 1 Truck of Sheepskin & Fur lined Coats rec'd and issued.	
"	23rd		1 Truck of Blankets received and issued.	
"	24th		4 Tons of Stores & 1 Watercart received and issued. Also 164 Bales of Boots rec'd.	
"	25th		6 " do received and issued.	
"	26th		No Stores received.	
"	27th		10,750 Blankets received to complete second Blanket per man	
"	28th		8 Tons of Stores received and issued. Moved to Lannoy.	
Lannoy	29th		No Stores received	
"	30th		5 Tons of Stores received and issued.	
"	31		No Stores received	

Geo Edwardes-Lawrence
Major
D.A.D.O.S. 40th Division

20/38.

D.A.A.G.
40th: Divi:

Herewith
Original copy of
War Diary for month
of November 1918 —

30/11/18.

Resilto
Couvrs
Jovareso
Hobin

WAR DIARY or INTELLIGENCE SUMMARY.

Army Form C. 2118.

(Erase heading not required.)

Place	Date 1918	Hour	Summary of Events and Information	Remarks and references to Appendices
Lannoy	Nov 1st		7 Tons of Stores received and issued.	
"	2nd		No Stores received.	
"	3rd		5 Tons of Stores received and issued.	
"	4th		8 " do do do.	
"	5th		No Stores received.	
"	6th		5 Tons of Stores received and issued.	
"	7th		1 " do do. also 3 Lewis guns.	
"	8th		9 " do do do 2 do do.	
"	9th		No Stores received	
"	10th		6 Tons of Stores received and issued.	
"	11th		3 " do do do.	
"	12th		5 " do do do.	
"	13th		No Stores received.	
"	14th		2 Tons of Stores received and issued.	
"	15th		6 " do do do	

Geo Edwardes-Lawrence
Major D.A.D.O.S.
40th Division

WAR DIARY
or
INTELLIGENCE SUMMARY
(Erase heading not required.)

Place	Date	Hour	Summary of Events and Information	Remarks and references to Appendices
Kemmel	Mar 16"		12 O/R's wounded	
"	17"		1 O/R's wounded and sick	
"	18"		1 O/R wounded	
"	19"		5 O/R's wounded and sick	
"	20"		10 O/R's wounded	
"	21"		11 O/R's wounded and sick	
"	22"		10 O/R's wounded	
"	23"		11 O/R's wounded and sick	
"	24"		10 O/R's wounded	
"	25"			
"	26"		6 O/R's wounded and sick. Burnt by Gerdaux	Rendezvous 27.4.28
"	27.4.28		10 O/R's wounded	
"	29"		5 O/R's wounded and sick	
"	30"		10 O/R's wounded	

Geo Edwards-Ferguson
Major
J.J.Q.S.
4th Division

WAR DIARY or INTELLIGENCE SUMMARY

Army Form C. 2118.

DADOS 40D
V831

Place	Date 1918	Hour	Summary of Events and Information	Remarks and references to Appendices
Roubaix	Dec 1st		4 Tons of Stores received and issued.	
"	2nd		No Stores received.	
"	3rd		5 Tons of Stores received and issued.	
"	4th		No Stores received.	
"	5th		8 Tons of Stores received and issued.	
"	6th		4 " do do do.	
"	7th		5 " do do do.	
"	8th		No Stores received.	
"	9th		5 Tons of Stores received and issued.	
"	10th		No Stores received.	
"	11th		9 Tons of Stores received and issued.	
"	12th		No Stores received.	
"	13th		10 Tons of Stores received and issued.	
"	14 & 15		No Stores received.	
"	16th		7 Tons of Stores received and issued.	

Leo Edwards Freeman
Major
D.A.D.O.S. 40. Division

WAR DIARY
or
INTELLIGENCE SUMMARY

Army Form C. 2118.

Place	Date	Hour	Summary of Events and Information	Remarks and references to Appendices
Barbara	1918 Oct 17th		No stores received	
	18th		3 tons of stores received and issued	
	19th		No stores received	
	20th		4 tons of stores received and issued	
	21st		No stores received	
	22nd		do do do	
	23rd		3 tons of stores received and issued	
	24th		9 " " " "	
	25th		No stores received	
	26th		10 tons of stores received and issued	
	27th 28		No stores received	
	29th		3 tons of stores received and issued	
	30th		6 " do do do	
	31st		No stores received	

Lt Quartermaster
Major & Adjt
4th " Division.

1st Sheet

WAR DIARY or INTELLIGENCE SUMMARY
(Erase heading not required.)

Army Form C. 2118

D.A.D.O.S. 40th Division

Vol 32

Place	Date	Hour	Summary of Events and Information	Remarks and references to Appendices
Roubaix	1-1-19		10 tons blankets received	
"	2-1-19		8 " " "	
"	3-1-19		1 " General Stores received	
"	4-1-19		4 " " " " "	
"	8-1-19		4 " " " " "	
"	9-1-19		6 " " " " "	
"	11-1-19		9 " " " " "	
"	14-1-19		6 " " " " "	
"	15-1-19		Major McPatrick arrived & assumed duties of D.A.D.O.S.	
"	15-1-19		5 tons Blankets received	
"	16-1-19		6 tons General Stores received	
"	18-1-19		D.A.D.O.S. visited G.O.C. 119th Inf. Brigade	
"	18-1-19		4 tons General Stores received	
"	20-1-19		7 " " " "	
"	21-1-19		6 " " " "	all Div
"	22-1-19		D.A.D.O.S. visited G.O.C. 120th Inf. Brigade; 39th M.G. Battn; Railhead; Div Coy Train	
"	22-1-19		3 tons General Stores received	
"	23-1-19		8 " " " "	
"	24-1-19		23 "wheels" received	
"	25-1-19		73 Boxes Horseshoes & 20 sack grindery & clothing received	

2nd Sheet

WAR DIARY
or
INTELLIGENCE SUMMARY
(Erase heading not required.)

Army Form C. 2118

Instructions regarding War Diaries and Intelligence Summaries are contained in F. S. Regs., Part II. and the Staff Manual respectively. Title Pages will be prepared in manuscript.

D·A·D·O·S
40th Division

Place	Date	Hour	Summary of Events and Information	Remarks and references to Appendices
Roubaix	25-1-19		D.A.D.O.S. visited G.O.C. 121st Inf Brigade: 224 Field Coy R.E.: Nos 2 & 3 Coys all Div. Train.	
"	27-1-19		6 tons General Stores received.	
"	28-1-19		5 " " " "	
"	29-1-19		D.A.D.O.S. visited C.R.A.: 64 A.F.A. Bde.: 229 Field Coy R.E.: 136 Field Amb.	

H. Patrick Major R.A.O.C.
D.A.D.O.S.
40th Division

WAR DIARY or INTELLIGENCE SUMMARY

Army Form C. 2118

ADOS. 40th Division   February 1919

Place	Date	Hour	Summary of Events and Information	Remarks and references to Appendices
Roubaix	1-2-19		One Body Kitchen Travelling received & issued	
"	2-2-19		Ten tons General Stores received & issued	
"	3-2-19		No stores received	
"	4-2-19		Seven tons General Stores received & issued	
"	6-2-19		Eight " " " " " "	
"	8-2-19		Three " " " " " "	
"	12-2-19		Eight " " " " " "	
"	12-2-19		Visited Artillery Headquarters & 136 Field Ambulance	
"	14-2-19		Eight tons General Stores received & issued	
"	15-2-19		Visited Div M.T. Coy	
"	16-2-19		" La Tombe Annual Camp	
"	20-2-19		Five tons General Stores received & issued	
"	22-2-19		Visited Headqrs 120 & 121 Brigades	
"	22-2-19		Five tons General Stores received & issued	
"	24-2-19		Visited 231 Field Coy R.E. & inspected equipment	
"	25-2-19		Ten tons General Stores received & issued	
"	27-2-19		Six tons General Stores received & issued	

Patrick Major
ADOS
40th Division

WAR DIARY
or
INTELLIGENCE SUMMARY
(Erase heading not required.)

Army Form C. 2118

Instructions regarding War Diaries and Intelligence Summaries are contained in F. S. Regs., Part II. and the Staff Manual respectively. Title Pages will be prepared in manuscript.

Dados.
40th Division   March 1919

Place	Date	Hour	Summary of Events and Information	Remarks and references to Appendices
Roubaix	1.3.19		Four tons General stores received & issued	
"	4.3.19		Three " " " " "	
"	7.3.19		Five " " " " " "	
"	11.3.19		Four " " " " " "	
"	14.3.19		Six " " " " " "	
"	18.3.19		Twelve. 18. pdr received & issued, Three for A Battery 64 Bde R.F.A, one for B. Btty 64 Bde R.F.A, one for A. Btty 181 Bde, two for B. Btty 181 Bde R.F.A, one for C/181 Bde R.F.A & two each for A & B. Bttys 178 Bde R.F.A	
			Four tons stores received & issued.	
"	31.3.19		Two " " " " "	
"	22.3.19		Seventy five pieces of Timber received & issued.	
"	25.3.19		Two Tons stores received & issued	
"	27.3.19		Six Tons " " " "	
"	28.3.19		Two " " " " "	

C.J. Page H/Condi.
R.A.O.S.
for Dados
40th Dn.

1875 Wt. W593/826 1,000,000 4/15 J.B.C. & A. A.D.S.S./Forms/C. 2118.

DADOS 40th Division   WAR DIARY or INTELLIGENCE SUMMARY   April 30th 1919   Army Form C. 2118.

DADOS 40 D

Place	Date	Hour	Summary of Events and Information	Remarks and references to Appendices
Roubaix	1-4-19		4 tons General Stores received and issued	VR 35
	2-4-19		1 " " " " " "	
	3-4-19		2 " " " " " "	
	4-4-19		3 " " " " " "	
	5-4-19		2 " " " " " "	
	7-4-19		5 " " " " " "	
	8-4-19		2 " " " " " "	
	10-4-19		2 " " " " " "	
	11-4-19		4 " " " " " "	
	14-4-19		6 " " " " " "	
	15-4-19		2 " " " " " "	
	18-4-19		2 " " " " " "	
	19-4-19		4 " " " " " "	
	22-4-19		75 pieces timber received & issued.	
	23-4-19		2 tons General Stores received and issued.	
	26-4-19		1 ton " " " " "	
	28-4-19		2 tons " " " " "	
	30-4-19		1 ton " " " " "	

A Patrick Major RAOC
DADOS
40th Division

30-4-19